Amy Grant

Amy Grant

A BIOGRAPHY
by
BOB MILLARD

A Dolphin Book

DOUBLEDAY & COMPANY, INC.
GARDEN CITY, NEW YORK
1986

Library of Congress Cataloging-in-Publication Data
Millard, Bob.
    Amy Grant: a biography.

    "A Dolphin book."
    1. Grant, Amy.
2. Gospel musicians—United States—Biography. I. Title.
ML420.G814M5   1986   784.5′0092′4 [B]   86-2125
ISBN 0-385-23470-8

Acknowledgments

The research and writing of this book about Amy Grant were made a great deal easier and more pleasurable by the assistance and encouragement of many people. Friends, family, industry sources, business associates, and fellow journalists gave generously of their time, talent, information, and moral support, the sum total of which represents the foundation upon which this volume was begun. There are so many people who introduced me to sources or steered me in the right direction that thanking everyone by name would take up many more pages than I am allotted for that purpose. For that support system of generous hearts that is the Nashville music and journalism community, I am very grateful.

Special thanks are due my wife, Lucinda Smith Millard, for her unflagging encouragement, understanding, and dogged, if painfully accurate, policing of the manuscript-in-progress, not to mention her constant faith in my abilities, which often exceeded my own. Dinners got cold while I pounded out "just one more paragraph," but the synergy of our relationship warmed me even in the cold days of rural Kentucky autumn, whence I finally retreated to complete my writing.

The spirit of cooperation and sharing that defines the

Nashville entertainment press corps and bonds entertainment reporters from many other corners of the country provided me with early and continued grist for the word mill. Few who need the validation that the printed and broadcast word gives to them appreciate the pressures and abuse under which these generous men and women grind out stories of their lives, concerts, and latest records. For opening their files to share information and lighten my research burden immensely, thanks to Robert K. Oermann *(Tennessean, USA Today)*, Don Cusic (Middle Tennessee State University), Ed Morris *(Billboard)*, Sandy Neese *(Tennessean)*, Ellis Widner (Tulsa *Tribune)*, the Nashville *Banner*, Pat Harris *(Time)*, Neil Pond *(Music City News)*, and WSMV-TV in Nashville for use of material from their "Dan Miller and Company" program. Other much appreciated research help came from Jeanne Carroll (Gospel Music Association), Dr. Robert Early and Dr. Herman Norton (Vanderbilt University Divinity School), Ronnie Pugh (Country Music Foundation Library), and the Metropolitan Nashville Public Library Nashville Room and main reference desk.

For unlimited photocopying privileges I am more deeply obliged to Frances Preston and CBS Records than either suspected would be the case when their generosity was extended. My stay at Carrico's Writers Retreat in Owensboro, Kentucky, allowed me the seclusion to concentrate on the final draft, not the least because the telephone refused to announce incoming calls.

I made some new friends among interview subjects and especially appreciate their recollections and opinions. Heartfelt thanks go to Don Butler, executive director of the Gospel Music Association; the Reverend Don Finto, pastor of Belmont Church; Wes Yoder, president and owner of Dharma Artist Agency; Dan Brock, manager of DeGarmo and Key; and Randy Cox, general manager of Meadowgreen Music. Thanks are due Andy Tolbird and Terry Short at Word Records/Nashville for the records, and to all the talented photographers whose pictures grace these pages.

Lastly, though their contributions began even before this project was formally undertaken, I wish to express my gratitude to Doubleday editor Jim Fitzgerald, assistant editor Casey Fuetsch, my agent Diana Price, my two hardworking packaging agents Madeleine Morel and Karen Moline of 2M Communications, and, of course, Amy Grant for making it all possible.

Introduction

Amy Grant's unprecedented rise from schoolgirl leading vesper sing-alongs to gospel music's top-selling act surprised a lot of people. Between the time she first entered a recording studio as a budding teenaged artist and the summer of 1985, when she became the first gospel artist to achieve certified sales of more than one million copies of a single album, Amy and her handlers had completely rewritten the book on commercial success by a gospel music singer. No gospel act had ever reached her heights or got to the top in the same way. Her successes in selling out major concert halls in such unlikely places as Los Angeles, Boston, and New York City caught just about everyone but Amy, her management team, and her fans completely off guard.

The vast majority of religious Americans had never heard of her, yet in mid-1983 the Recording Industry Association of America (RIAA) tracked the sale of the five hundred thousandth copy of her album "Age to Age" and presented her with the first gold record ever received by a solo contemporary Christian artist. Despite widely broadcast religious radio hits such as "El Shaddai," "Sing Your Praise to the Lord," and "Father's Eyes," Amy Grant was not a household name to the average guy on the street the way pop music million-sellers such as Michael Jackson, Billy Joel, or Barbra Streisand are. Even with a growing accumulation of Dove Awards from the prestigious Gospel Music Association, she was also something of an outsider to the gospel music industry.

Who is this sparkling beauty who breaks the rules of both the pop and gospel music worlds? Who is this outspoken young lady who speaks her mind boldly in religious-music magazines and the Bible of rock 'n' roll, *Rolling Stone,* as well as on religious TV and with NBC's Jane Pauley on the "Today" show? Who is this young woman who seems totally oblivious to the wisdom of past experience regarding what fans will and will not tolerate in their musical heroes, yet who emerges as a major force to be contended with in secular as well as Christian music markets?

Amy Grant may have become the most idealized American teenager since Ricky Nelson and Pat Boone. Boone, who drank milk and made even Little Richard's "Tutti Frutti" acceptable to the conservative "older generation," was one of the first to develop a "clean teen" cult in rock 'n' roll's wild and woolly heyday. Nelson was the youngest son of Ozzie Nelson, a bandleader in his prime, and singer Harriet Nelson. He found fame playing himself on his family's television show, "The Adventures of Ozzie and Harriet," in the 1950s and 1960s. He was as tepid as tea and toast compared to Elvis, but he was cute in his late teens and became another milk-drinking heartthrob singing light uptempo rock tunes and ballads to puppy love–struck kids of the first rock generation. Until his death in December 1985, Ricky Nelson's most scandalous feat as a teen idol was to drop out of the family television series and later divorce his wife, who had appeared on the show. Yet Amy, now in her mid-twenties, makes no bones about it that, despite her deep and committed religious faith, she is no goody two-shoes.

Amy Grant isn't shaped by other people's musical and philosophical biases. Borrowing melodies and rhythms from up-to-the-minute dance hits, reggae, and hard rock, she refuses to be a one-dimensional singer/songwriter. Choosing to wear leopard-skin jackets on stage, or go naked on South African beaches, she isn't limited by the expected image of a gospel singer, much less a Christian stamped out of a public image machine like some plastic dashboard icon. Aside from the quality of her music, it is her forthrightness about her human weaknesses, doubts, and pleasures as well as her matter-of-fact confession of faith that stands her on such solid ground with the teens and young adults who comprise the base of her still-expanding audience. Her composite honesty has made her a role model.

Amy is not quickly understood by someone unfamiliar with the polite, self-effacing aggressiveness of the genteel Southern gentry, a breed of go-getters who instinctively say please and thank you, but are unaccustomed to taking no for an answer. Nor is she any less a riddle to someone not actively involved in the consuming mysteries of personal miracles and the expectation of active participation of the Lord in day-to-day life found in Charismatic Christianity. Yet, her music and stage message are clear clarion calls to a growing segment of American youth whose concerns mingle such anxieties of adolescence as pimples, peer pressure, and puppy-love heartbreak with the first serious questions of religious faith.

Amy has been called "the Michael Jackson of gospel music" and "the Madonna of gospel rock," but neither appellation is a particularly apt metaphor. Jackson and Madonna are multimillion record sellers, as Amy has become, but success alone is their main claim to fame. Their significance to their musical genre is minimal outside the context of their gross income. Jackson has his sequined glove and patented moonwalk dance step. Madonna mixes her fashion metaphors with crosses hanging from the underwear which often highlights her stage costume. They have easily identifiable sounds and images, but neither is a pioneer. Neither has taken popular music anywhere it couldn't already go in the sense of crossing boundaries at risk, breaking ground that not only has never been successfully plowed, but is littered with land mines as well.

These artists, with whom Amy Grant has been compared, share the elements of currency and popularity, but they and their producers have simply homed in on trends in popular music. Amy has done that and more.

Amy Grant dances and bounces across the stage, youthful and energetic. If her album covers portray a sexy image, there is no overt sensuality in her stage appearance beyond that which is suggested by the aura of her healthy beauty and happiness. Where Madonna's songs address the overtly sensual aspects of lovemaking or being "a material girl," Amy embodies the sweet sex appeal of the Ivory soap girl. The difference becomes obvious when Amy begins belting out lyrics ranging from gospel praise exposition of "Angels" to morally conservative and emotionally encouraging "Wise Up" or "Who to Listen To."

The message is usually simple: Resist temptation, life gets tough but God is only a prayer away, love your spouse, get religion involved in your everyday life, forgive yourself, and have a good time. It's all high volume, high energy, high intensity, and by its success it is something entirely new to the gospel and pop scenes. One must go back further than the 1980s to find a meaningful comparison to Amy's phenomenon. She has unselfconsciously combined sounds and styles that were formerly regarded as antithetical by pop and gospel establishments alike. Listeners may recall a singing phenomenon who began in 1954, a young, swaggering artist of unconscious sexual explosiveness, also a child of Tennessee, who tore down barriers to blend musical styles. His name: Elvis Presley.

With his slurred, raw vocalizing and undeniable sex appeal, Presley meshed the rhythms of electric urban black music with redneck country rockabilly and turned the world of popular music upside down. His personal magnetism gave form to a previously unarticulated restlessness of post-WW II teens. He pulled off a combination of musical cultures, the effects of which still dominate the pop music scene thirty years later.

Elvis, being a son of the fundamentalist South, loved church music and recorded a number of albums of hymns with the Jordanaires, the same backup vocal quartet that added the hum-a-hum-a-doo-wop to most of his early rock hits, lending celestial gospel harmonies. This only came after his rock success was firmly established, however. His street-level sexy gyrations and makeup-enhanced bedroom eyes marked him, even on his gospel record covers, as a most desirable young man.

There is an unmistakable desirability about Amy Grant, too. Her beauty is created in large part by her frizzy, flowing tresses and compelling big eyes that can make that personal connection even with back-row fans. It is, peculiarly, a sexiness without reference to sex itself. She has a clean kind of animal magnetism that says sex appeal to some people and big-sister strength to others. That characteristic of appearing to be many good things to many different people is the magic dust of stardom. No artist can buy it, learn it, or otherwise create that one element if it isn't naturally there. Elvis had it and so does Amy Grant, though his poor Mississippi childhood and Memphis-tenement teen years were a far cry from Amy's upbringing as part of the elite of Nashville's richest, best, and brightest.

But Elvis didn't invent rock 'n' roll, he popularized it. He was the focal point of its initial breakthrough to repressed white teenagers. Amy has similarly been the biggest single force behind mass-audience recognition of gospel's contemporary Christian subgenre. Of course, Elvis in his early days was seen by fans' parents as dangerously working class, feral, and (in their mistaken perception) antiestablishment. "White trash" was the common early adult judgment of The Pelvis. Amy, on the other hand, is well scrubbed, upper middle class, and so clearly representative of Southern Yuppie sensibilities that she was honored in her senior year at Harpeth Hall School as the girl who most embodied the values of Nashville's most exclusive girls school.

Amy Grant is a powerful and unlikely force in both the Christian and secular pop marketplaces today. She admits that she was in the proverbial "right place at the right time" to ride the crest of contemporary Christian music's growing popularity, but she brought a uniqueness of philosophy, personality, and talent that have made her accomplishments possible. Her story is one of strong family ties, youth in rebellion against long-established hierarchy of a Southern fundamentalist religious denomination, confidence and insecurities, and music mixed with romance mixed in turn with one of the most explosively powerful religious movements of the second half of the twentieth century.

How she made use of her talents and charisma, often without seeming to have any conscious thoughts of stardom as a goal, makes a fascinating tale about an artist who continues to expand the limits of gospel music.

Amy Grant

Chapter 1

Amy Lee Grant was born in Augusta, Georgia, on November 25, 1960, only a few weeks after handsome war hero and Massachusetts Senator Jack Kennedy turned youth, charisma, and the backing of a wealthy family into key elements of his narrow presidential victory over Richard Nixon. Characteristics and advantages that helped carry Kennedy over the top would come into play for Amy as she started her climb to stardom in her mid-teen years.

"I was born at St. Joseph Hospital (in Augusta)," Amy says. "My dad was doing his residency there. We moved when I was six months old."

Her father, Dr. Burton Paine Grant, is still a practicing radiologist, a specialist in cancer treatment. He followed his own father, Dr. Otis Grant, into medicine and did his internship at Vanderbilt Hospital and the Veterans Administration in Nashville. He had taken his young family, then comprised of wife Gloria and young daughters, Mimi and Kathy, from Nashville to Augusta in 1956. For the first two of the five years he spent in Augusta he was assigned to the army hospital at Fort Gordon. The Grant family grew during that residence in Georgia. They added two more daughters, first Carol then Amy, before Dr. Grant's medical duties and training took them to Houston, Texas, in 1961, then finally back to Nashville to set up his permanent medical practice.

The Grant family is deeply religious and more than comfortably well off. Theirs is one of the third-generation households of business and professional people whose importance in Nashville's business community and society arose not only from their own accomplishments, but from those of their forefathers; in Amy's family's case, those of her great grandfather, insurance multimillionaire and noted philanthropist A. M. Burton. Dr. Burton Grant's mother was one of six children of A. M. Burton. The patriarch of that close-knit and prominent Nashville family had achieved his status as had nearly all of Tennessee's original indigenous aristocracy—he earned it through his own success in business. Public achievement in the family line continued even into the fourth generation. Burton great grandchildren, cousins of Amy's generation, include Wilson Burton, a founder of the city magazine, *Nashville*, and former Vanderbilt University football star kicker Barry Burton.

In fact, the Burton family has been one of *the* important families in Nashville's business and religious circles for much of this century. Amy's great grandfather, Andrew Mizell Burton was a self-made man, a shining example of the traditional American success story. Born just fourteen years after the Civil War on a farm in Trousdale County, Tennessee, he was eighteen years old when he walked into Nashville for the first time, leading a cow.

He must have sold the cow, for within a week he was digging ditches and working at other hard manual labor as a carpenter's helper on the construction crew for the 1897 Tennessee Centennial Exposition. The young Andy Burton was sober, enterprising, and frugal, a paragon of the Puritan work ethic. He walked three miles to work each day to save carfare and managed to save half of his dollar-per-day wages toward his future, whatever that might be.

When the construction job ran out, Burton took his first job as a salesman in the insurance industry. Within six years he had become the youngest president of an insurance company in the nation. With $1,000 of his own savings and an equal amount from a partner, Burton founded the Life & Casualty Insurance Company (now part of the American General Life Insurance Company megalith) and built it into one of the biggest insurers in the South. He retired from the helm in 1951, after forty-eight years of active management. Her grandfather, Andy

Burton was a member of the staunchly conservative Church of Christ, and his religion bolstered his upwardly mobile Southern values of thrift and hard work. Although he had only twenty months' formal education when he arrived in Nashville, Burton educated himself through constant reading. He continually added the ideas of inspirational and motivational thinkers to his own bootstrap, success-directed values. He tied biblical exhortations to the work ethic by attending open lectures at the Church of Christ's main institution of higher learning, David Lipscomb College in Nashville. He was an ardent reader and enjoyed expounding upon his philosophical discoveries in weekly columns for the L&C company newsletter, *The Mirror.* These columns were later collected and edited in two volumes of self-improvement essays called *Gleanings.* Burton penned at least two other books, short correlations between the Bible and church teachings. These volumes, while not considered part of the doctrinal writings of the church, illuminate Burton's own considerable feelings about the importance of spreading knowledge of church teachings and positions.

He not only wrote about his religion and its relation to America's best values, as he saw them, he put his money where his mouth was. During his lifetime A. M. Burton gave more than $15 million to charitable causes, primarily to Christian education. During his lifetime, as much as $4 million went to David Lipscomb College alone. Gifts totaling about $500,000 reportedly saved the college from ruin when a series of dormitory fires during the winter of 1929–30 threatened to put it out of business. That half million dollar sum may not sound so big now, but that was the beginning of the Great Depression, a time when $100 per month was a handsome salary for many white-collar workers.

Upon his death at eighty-seven in 1966, Burton willed his 109-acre Burton Farm to the college in life estate trust for his wife Lillie May Armstrong Burton. The farm was located in fashionable, yet at that time sparsely developed, Green Hills area of Davidson County. It consisted of an expansive, hilly, and wooded acreage less than ten miles from downtown Nashville, yet quite luxuriously rural. Many members of the family fought a public tooth-and-nail battle against what they felt was shabby treatment of their matriarch, accusing the college administration of letting Mrs. Burton's home and the property go to seed. By the time Mrs. Burton died in 1981, the college was more strapped for cash than for expansion acreage, so the land was sold for residential development, retaining the name Burton Hills. That development of high-priced, densely-packed condos, townhouses, apartments, and office buildings got under way in the summer of 1985.

Burton Farm was the common heritage of the children, grandchildren, and great grandchildren of A. M. Burton and Miss Lillie May. Amy Grant was just one of dozens of great grandchildren who spent much of their childhood riding horses, hiking, swimming in ponds, and playing hide-and-seek on the Burton Farm. The inspiration and love that Amy drew from her great grandmother resulted in a song she penned called "Mimi's House."

The memory of childhood pleasures on that property were offset for many of the descendants of A. M. Burton when controversies continually arose between the college and the family over what was perceived as the Lipscomb College's poor stewardship of the Burton property during his widow's lifetime. Amy got over any hard feelings that may have developed over that incident and the later sale, which some in the family also opposed. She remembers mostly the good times on Burton Farm, a special place indeed.

"Hey, I grew up on that farm," Amy says. "I didn't actually. My great grandmother and great grandfather lived on that farm. Actually, it's being developed. My great grandparents willed it to a college here in town. . . . We were just excited that they named it Burton Hills because we grew up riding horses and our whole family had a street on the back of the farm that my great grandparents gave us. It was all cousins. It was fun. I have great memories . . ."

In addition to great grandmother Mimi's attentions, the rest of the Grant family lavished love and attention on their youngest daughter, instilling in her a tremendous sense of self-worth.

"Well, I was the baby of the family, and that probably says a lot," she told local television interviewer Dan Miller. "Much more [attention] than I deserved. I mean, I thought I was the funniest thing that had ever hit this earth. My family made me feel so confident. Then I got to first grade and I did all my huh-ahuh-huh—nobody laughed. I wasn't funny! I was warped. My parents used to tease and say they ought to sell tickets to dinner, because they thought I was funny.

"You know, so many wonderful things that were horrible when I was younger really helped me learn to laugh at myself [and] have really helped me in the public eye. I wet the bed until I was in the fifth grade. You'd spend the night out and you'd have to tell your friend, 'Well, your dog climbed in bed with me and he had an accident.' You go through this long thing and they'd say they didn't have a dog. It's hard when you're little. My family really helped me to learn to laugh."

There was encouragement and a little bit of creative spoiling for Amy, but her earliest musical experiences came as a matter of course through the family worship practices. The Grants regularly attended their local Church of Christ, where Amy's introduction to church music came through stern hymns, sung a cappella because the sect eschews instrumental music in the sanctuary.

"I wouldn't call it unjoyful. I would call it very simple, at least in the sound," Amy has illuminated. "In the Church of Christ there is no instrumental music, but we used to sing loud and long and hard and joyfully."

Amy took her first piano lesson when she was ten years old, but she didn't devote a lot of long, hard study to the instrument. Her interests ran more to a friendly game of basketball with neighborhood kids, and she was developing a healthy interest in the popular recording artists of the day. Her favorite artists were soft rock, folk, and pop artists, though she had fairly undiscriminating tastes in music. She liked all kinds, whatever she was exposed to. For the most part, the rebel music of contemporary Christian artists of that time never entered her world of religious orthodoxy.

Whatever additional musical influences there may have been in the Grant household when Amy was growing up seem, from Amy's recollections, to have been fairly limited and arcane.

"My parents were not real musical," she recalls. "They [still] are not. My father sings a lot, but . . . We sang, but the songs we sang in our house were not hit songs. I can't figure out what it was we listened to, exactly."

Amy's childhood was a normal, if privileged one. She says she was a rambunctious and often rebellious grammar school student who often wound up in the principal's office at the Ensworth private grammar school. By the time she and her girlfriends reached the threshold of adolescence in the seventh grade, Amy was already very self-conscious about her appearance. She wanted to fit in and was disappointed when she was surpassed in early physical development by some of her classmates. She first noticed the changes when some of the girls in her private school physical education class began turning into "seventh-grade Raquel Welches."

"Seventh grade is about the time when kids start to smell bad [after exercising in gym class]," Amy explains. "So after sweating for about forty-five minutes we had to go shower. We were at the age where everyone is curious. We all looked around and checked each other out. It seemed like everybody's body was changing but mine."

No matter how much she wished for puberty to come on like gangbusters, Amy was fated by heredity to wait a little longer than some of the other girls. Always a take-charge type, Amy talked her mother into ironing the frizzy curls out of her hair every day so she could wear her hair in the popular, long, straight, center-parted style of the time. Amy's widow's-peak hairline, always one of the most compelling features of her natural beauty, made such a hair style nearly impossible for her.

"I had this outrageously curly hair with a widow's peak—a couple of cowlicks that meet in the middle of your forehead, and it looks like a cheap Dracula movie. One day in school, I went into the bathroom and with a lot of spit and two-thirds of my hair ironed I was able to put the part in the middle. I felt great. I strutted back into study hall and this girl named Rachael says, 'Wow! Amy, you look like Eddie Munster.'"

Eddie Munster, son of a comic Frankenstein in the popular 1960s television series "The Munsters," had an exaggerated Wolfman-style widow's peak. He was not, of course, the kind of character a young girl striving hard for "the mod look" would want to be compared with. Amy borrowed her father's shaving razor, secreted herself in her bathroom at home, and removed the offending hairline.

"It was great, except the next day was a nightmare," she recalls. "My first five-o'clock shadow. For ten days I took an extra fifteen minutes before school to iron my hair and shave my forehead."

Her junior high vanity came to her mother's attention immediately, but Gloria Grant tolerated Amy's experiment in depilatory science for a few days before confronting her about the missing widow's peak.

"I had to be honest because mothers know everything," Amy says, with a glint of humor. "I said, 'Mom, it fell off!' "

The widow's peak returned soon thereafter.

A loving toleration of their daughter's growing pains was coupled with a pervasive emphasis on God's place in the family. The Grant's are intensely religious. There was as likely to be a Psalter as a salt shaker on the family dining table. Amy's parents had inculcated her and her sisters with a strong sense of God as an integral part of their family and individual lives.

"We read Bible stories to our children from the time they were a year old," Amy's mother, Gloria, says. "We had Bible verses and Bible songs at the breakfast table, but we never had a strict situation that would make them rebel against it. What we wanted most to instill in our girls was for each of them to have a desire to know God through His Son, Jesus Christ, and to have a personal relationship with Him. All we could do was plant this desire. You can't make people do things."

Grant family evangelism was not limited to their own brood, either. One neighbor reports having been proselytized by Gloria Grant when he was a child. "I got the idea that we were going to hell if we didn't believe like they did," he said. Even Amy sometimes wanted to rebel against her parents' strict Church of Christ views.

"We went to church [but] there were times when I

thought I wanted to figure it out for myself and balked at my parents," she told *Time* magazine interviewer Pat Harris. "I remember coming home from school and just thinking about life and looking at trees."

Amy grew in her religious commitment, and, during her seventh-grade year, she volunteered for baptism at the family Church of Christ congregation that year. She had complete emersion in a chilly baptismal pool, in keeping with the sect's teaching of adult rather than infant baptism. It was at about that same time, at the leading edge of puberty, that she began to take up the guitar.

"When I first started to play guitar I knew about four chords and I squeezed every song I knew into those four chords," Amy has said. "I sang early Elton John, Carole King, James Taylor, John Denver, acoustic-sounding songs.

"There were a lot of things happening in my life then," she said. "I went through all the usual growing-up pain: severe acne, braces on my teeth, Coke-bottle eyeglasses, crushes . . ."

Thus, at the beginning of adolescence, Amy Grant was hit by an increasing interest in music, hormones, and the Holy Spirit. Some major influences had begun to emerge.

Chapter 2

Interest in boys and her initial Charismatic Christian experience came to Amy at about the same time. These concurrent developments of puberty and increased piety probably had a lot to do with shaping Amy's personal beliefs. That combination, added to an attitude of tolerance which her parents instilled in the impressionable teen, seem to have led her to public acclamations that being a Christian young woman in the eighties is "sexy."

Amy is certainly not the first person to apply sex appeal to a gospel music persona. Black gospel singers often retain an electric sensuality in their musical ministry. One example is the Reverend Al Green, a popular soul singer in the sixties. Green has since become a singing minister in Memphis, where he works his congregation into quite a lather of enthusiasm with his legendary stage sex appeal, creating gospel fervor out of the sizzling ecstasy his movements and vocalizations still conjure.

Amy has none of that kind of hot and howling sensuality, but she is one of the first white gospel singers to incorporate songs of man/woman love into her performance. The lyrics to one of her 1985 pop-charting records, "Find a Way," address the heartbreak of lost love, while "I Love You" calls her husband a prince charming and talks of the comfort of true love with no reference whatsoever to religion. Many of the tunes she wrote for her album "Unguarded" reveal her belief that Christian-aimed music can and should deal with human feelings and relationships from the perspective of Christian individuals, though not always mentioning the deity. This is not a theme found widely in gospel music prior to her emergence on the scene. But it is one that she has been nursing in one way or another on all her albums. Amy seems to have avoided one of the most common perceptions of Southern fundamentalist religions, that sex is dirty, that things of the body are inherently sinful. In fact, the whole subject of sin is almost entirely absent from her music.

Amy's attitude about a nonexclusive relationship between religion and such everyday human realities as physical love, grandparents, and humor comes as much from her economic and social class as from her religious background. Amy is willing to go public with her attitudes about such things, often making observations that show her to be closer to mainstream America than to the discrete public silence on such topics that comes from most quarters of the gospel music community. It is possible that such a son of the Pentecostal South as Jerry Lee Lewis might have been much less self-destructive had he not been haunted in his own penchant for wine, women, pills, and songs that praise the same by the fundamentalist religious teaching of his childhood that pleasures of the flesh are always sinful.

Amy is certainly no sexpot on stage, but her song lyrics may help people to enjoy sensual pleasures without guilt— at the proper time and place, of course. Such themes in her music have drawn criticism from her most conservative detractors as being unfit for gospel music, whether or not they are presented within a rock music framework, which they also reject.

Singing songs about loving one's spouse, or other equally pedestrian life-style commentaries would hardly draw reproach for any artist whose home base was not in the world of religious music. Any number of gospel acts have learned the hard way that private lives and public appearances, including espoused attitudes, don't have to match as long as fans don't find out. Alcoholism, illicit sex, and drug abuse occur within certain corners of the gospel community probably as much as in any other segment of the entertainment field. When child-molestation charges were brought against a member of contemporary Christian rock group White Heart in 1985, it shook the industry with feelings of outrage and sympathy. The band member was quietly dropped and the band continued on. Actually, gospel fans are usually very forgiving of an artist who is caught straying, as long as he or she gives an obligatory repentance at concerts for a period thereafter. No one held black contemporary gospel star André Crouch's early eighties cocaine bust against him for long.

Amy Grant raises the ire of some segments of the Christian community not because her personal behavior is immoral—it isn't. If anything, her personal standards are slightly to the right of most people's idea of upright. She riles them because she voices opinions that, while tame to secular tastes, tap, with almost liberating force, a yearning for a role model by those who wish to live by Christian values without the burden of religious guilt. She speaks for many middle-class teens and young adults on that score.

"I think she wants to say that it's okay to be a Christian and have fun," explains husband Gary Chapman. "Not to completely separate yourself from humanity just because you don't believe exactly like everyone else."

Amy's outspokenness on such subjects extends, remarkably for a gospel singer, to recreational drugs at her concerts. Her point is not approval, or disapproval. She rarely accepts public responsibility for judging other people. Her thrust in this area is against hypocrisy, an attitude that is encouraging in an age group already prone to rebellion against parental and church authority.

"I remember years ago—it sounds so mundane now—the first time I smelled somebody smoking a joint at a concert, I was thrilled," Amy remembers. "I thought, this is incredible. Not that there aren't some Christians that smoke pot—yes, it does exist—but it meant to me that obviously this person is not affected by the church peer pressure. A lot of people smoke like smokestacks, but if they're in a gathering that they know is all Christians, they will not totally be themselves."

Amy was totally herself during her high school days, which meant there was plenty of religious input then. It was in her first year at Harpeth Hall high school that she began making her own discoveries about God, moving beyond her early church schooling. As she started growing from little girl to young lady, her interest in boys was not muted by the uniformed, all-girl-campus atmosphere. Her teen-aged experiments with sex were mainly teasing little escapades. Amy was always in control.

"Petting happens," she admitted. "It's part of growing up, finding out who you are, how men and women work. As a teenager, when I gave part of me to someone, I knew I was just going to flirt, have a little fun, and do whatever I could rationalize, but go no further, because there is only one first time."

Her interest in having a boyfriend led her to discover the Church of Christ Charismatics when her puppy-love crush on a young man nine years her senior motivated her to accept an older sister's invitation to her first Bible study meeting. That meeting was a turning point for Amy.

"That happened when I was a freshman in high school," Amy said. "The guy reading it [the Bible] was dating my older sister. I thought he was the cutest thing that had ever happened in Nashville. He was nine years older than me and I thought, 'Mimi, I hate to do this to you, but I'm going to steal this guy away.' So I went to this Bible study thinking I was going to make this guy fall in love with me.

"I was fourteen. Hey, you know. But I was so over-whelmed by what they were talking about at this Bible study. I became a very serious, committed Christian. I mean, fourteen is young, but it just hit me. As a result of that, I never stopped singing the old songs, but when you sing, part of the joy of singing is that you're singing from your own experience. You can take an Elton John love song and sing it when you're in junior high and your boyfriend broke up with you. You're singing it with all the passion you can muster. But there were a lot of things happening in my life, emotionally and spiritually, that I didn't have any songs to relate to. So I went back in my room at night and thought, 'Okay, to round out my repertoire, what can I write?' "

Part of Amy's own attraction to that early Bible study group was her feelings of claustrophobia at being under her parents' watchful eye at church. It was an outgrowth of the normal teenaged rebellion that takes many forms at this stage in a young person's life, when asserting one's individual identity becomes of paramount importance. Naturally, Amy's spiritual prairie fire turned its heat toward Dr. and Mrs. Grant in the same way that adolescent discovery of any verity of life is often turned to reproach of one's parents.

"I was pretty much a good kid," Amy remembers. "But, when I left my parents' church and went searching on my own I thought I was rebelling in the biggest way. It felt good. When you're young and discover any sort of truth, it suddenly makes you want to tell your parents how to live. They must have been trying to keep a straight face. Every parent must go through it."

Her penchant for singing pop songs as well as gospel tunes is an extension of her continued insistence on asserting her individuality within an industry that traditionally disapproves of "crossover" attempts. Her continued ability to tap and share the intensity of those feelings is a key to Amy's acceptance by her youthful audiences.

Amy underwent a change in her religious beliefs during her high school years. Her religious fervor was intensified by the stimulation of new ideas she was getting from the Bible study group. Perhaps it is because the conservative Southern Church of Christ teachings from her childhood converged with ideas from the Charismatic movement when she was in her early adolescence that her message is heard so clearly by youngsters in their teens. Because the religious influences in her life are key to her career and music, they deserve a closer look.

Raised within the most conservative and Southern wing of a movement called the Disciples of Christ, which was begun in frontier America in the early 1800s, Amy received a religious education that proclaimed the Churches of Christ the only legitimate heir to pre-Catholic first- and second-century Christianity. Some Church of Christ congregations even go so far as to proclaim that direct connection with original Christianity by chiseling "Founded, A.D. 33" into the cornerstone of their houses of worship. The church professes as a core belief that the New Testament is the sole source of doctrinal and practical authority, with adult baptism as its only sacrament. The Churches of Christ split from the other sects descended from the Disciples of Christ coalition more on the basis of disagreements on how things should be done, rather than over basic Christian doctrine.

As a child, Amy would have been exposed to the pervasive Church of Christ idea that its religious practices, drawn from New Testament scripture references, was the only path to heaven. It is an exclusivist idea that, unfortunately for ecumenicism, is shared by a number of other Christian denominations. Each, of course, excludes the other from salvation as a means of strengthening its hold on its members and as a tool for recruiting members of other churches. At any rate, Amy was taught that there was only "one way" to heaven, an idea that can cause great anguish for those who find the teachings somehow at odds with their own faith. Luckily, when Amy at fourteen began to seek knowledge of a Charismatic faith, she found such a movement beginning to take shape within the loose organizational framework of the Church of Christ.

Amy's childhood faith taught one sacrament, emersion of adults in baptism, but recommended five additional "commands of God" which carried only slightly less weight than sacraments. Those are singing (a cappella due to a lack of mention of instrumentation in New Testament exhortations to "make a joyful noise"), preaching, praying, charitable giving, and partaking of the Lord's Supper. She accompanied the devout Grant family to three services a week, Sunday morning, Sunday evening, and Wednesday evening, in addition to periodic week-long evening revivals preached by traveling ministers.

Her Church of Christ background was quite at odds with full-blown Charismatic Christianity, which formed the basis for the religion of Amy's teen years and adulthood. Local believers managed to merge tenets of Charismatic Christianity with basic Church of Christ beliefs to form the practices and teachings of Amy's present religious home, the Belmont Church.

The Greek word "charisma" means "gift." Scholars suggest most charismatics of the eighties consider their experience one of spiritual renewal rather than one of radical departure from their previous religion. Borrowing from poor white Southern Pentecostalism such elements as glossolalia (speaking in tongues), faith healing, and other personal miracles as outward signs of salvation, a more subtle movement called Charismatic Christianity began to find adherents among the middle classes in the early 1960s. Because such activities are often subject to ridicule by outsiders, Belmont Church members are not in the habit of identifying which of their fellows have been visited by such Spirit gifts. It is, therefore, not known what personal experience, if any, Amy and her family have had with the healing or other aspects of their faith.

The Charismatic Christian movement started out small, as a rebellion against staid liturgical denominations, but gained credence among a wider number of Americans. A Gallup poll in 1978 showed that about 12.5 percent of American Christians identified themselves as Charismatics.

In quiet, conservative Nashville, headquarters for the Church of Christ, the Baptist Sunday School Board, the United Methodist Publishing House, the Board of Discipleship, and the Board of Higher Education and Ministry, this movement during the late sixties found fertile ground in David Lipscomb College professor and Church of Christ minister Don Finto. At odds with the Church of Christ in 1971, Finto became the pastor of Amy's Belmont Church. He is a tall man, with thick silver hair framing his balding pate. His sparkling eyes and friendly manner instantly put people at ease. His warmth, strength of character, and tireless involvement in outreach and social ministries in Nashville and the near-ghetto neighborhood surrounding Music Row have won him respect even among those who disagree with him theologically. His conversion to a Charismatic faith was the instigating factor in the process that in fourteen years changed the dwindling, elderly Belmont Church of Christ into the more than 1,600-member Belmont Church Christian Assembly, to which Amy Grant and many other Nashville-based contemporary Christian artists belong.

"When the whole Charismatic movement broke onto the scene, we all had to face that," Finto says. "And though I have never been fully gung ho into what is generally called the 'Charismatic movement,' I am Charismatic biblically because I believe in the fullness of the Spirit and the full gifts of the Spirit."

Finto, whose beliefs conflicted with Church of Christ orthodoxy, left his position as head of the Language Department at David Lipscomb College in Nashville. He was soon called by friends to become the preacher at what was then the Belmont Church of Christ. According to Finto, that congregation was already varying from typical conservative practices of the Churches of Christ, especially in the realm of race relations. The Belmont congregation welcomed blacks, disillusioned students, and newly converted "Christian hippies" who haunted the streets of downtown Nashville at different times during that period. To this liberal trend Finto began to add his dynamism and his Spirit-filled theology.

"It was different," Finto recalls. "We had no dress code at a time when most churches had dress codes. We accepted people regardless of what their problems were. We didn't condone, but we accepted in order to try to help people. We had a lot of outreach kinds of things and we were just getting criticized a lot."

Finto also brought to the tiny congregation, whose plain sanctuary seemed at first to swallow up the barely seventy members still clinging to the inner-city church, a substantial number of Lipscomb students with whom he had been involved in Bible study groups and counseling. He walked a thin line for years before breaking with the Church of Christ completely. He has still not legally surrendered the name Belmont Church of Christ, though the congregation stopped hanging out that shingle around 1980, identifying itself as the Belmont Church, a Christian Assembly, or the Belmont Assembly.

"We sort of became the Jesus church of this city," Finto explains. "We were still an institutional church so we had some degree of credibility. We also had some older people here that kept somewhat of a balance. One of the men who was an elder then is an elder now—he's over eighty. He received the barefoot people and he received the blue-jeans and overalls people, the long-haired people. He was open enough somehow to be able to accept people."

Finto worked with such energetic and influential Belmont Church youths as Dan Harrell, described by Finto at the time as "one of our hippie youth leaders." Harrell married Amy's older sister Kathy, who invited her sister Mimi to Belmont, who in turn invited sister Amy at the age of thirteen. Amy's introduction to Finto's style of religion came in part because she was beginning a stage of adolescent rebellion against her parents. Again, it was the Holy Ghost and hormones that dictated Amy's move to the Belmont Church, but she actually went with her parents' blessing.

"It was the biggest result of feeling uncomfortable going to church with my family," Amy confessed to Nashville newspaper reporter Sandy Neese. "The idea of my parents, who knew every scummy thing about me, watching me pray in church, watching me move to my knees. I had a hard time."

Amy, for whom religion was as much a part of her being as her rapidly changing body, strived to assert her identity as an individual in her own right. That process would necessarily include establishing her own path of faith in which to walk. The strength of her family's historic involvement in the Church of Christ virtually assured that she would not consciously stray far afield. The Bahai, Buddhist, and transcendental meditation movements were among Eastern religions that had active flocks in Nashville at that time, but attending the most liberal Church of Christ in town would suffice for young Amy.

Charismatic Christian teachings can be quite direct and emotionally exhilarating to someone searching for emotional content in religion. Its message of a joyful personal salvation and the beliefs relating to Holy Spirit powers coming to the faithful are electrifying to a hungry and searching mind, as Amy Grant's was at fourteen. The energy exuded by the group captivated her.

"I thought whatever it is that makes them so different, I've got to have it, too," she explains.

To the extent that Amy Grant's gospel music career embodies a ministry, it is directed primarily at young people who are vulnerable and searching as she was at that time in her life. She took her new faith and motivation to heart and began to keep watch for opportunities to share it.

"I wasn't the kind of person that became a Christian and started throwing a Bible around," she recalls. "When people are hurting it's so easy to say, 'This will help.' The hard thing is when people are sitting around—how can I broach the subject?"

She would find ample opportunity to develop those sharing skills as she plunged into the exhilarating atmosphere of one of the city's finest academic atmospheres for teen-aged girls—Harpeth Hall School.

Chapter 3

Harpeth Hall, Nashville's most exclusive girl's school, received Amy as one of its own. The school is nestled on twenty-six acres deep in the hilly suburb of Green Hills, on the edge of the prestigious Belle Meade community where the Grant family resides. From the original entrance gate, Harpeth Hall's school buildings are hidden from view from the road by magnificent old oaks, magnolias, and evergreens. Within its campus is a top-notch middle school and high school. The school's educational philosophy evolves in part from that of its predecessor, historic Ward-Belmont School, a "finishing school" for the daughters of Southern gentry until it passed out of existence in 1951.

Because Harpeth Hall is noted for giving plenty of growing room and encouragement to girls with talent and leadership abilities, Dr. and Mrs. Grant could not have picked a better environment for Amy. They had already sent her older sisters, Kathy, Mimi, and Carol to the noted private girls school before her. Among other outstanding students at the school during Amy's era there was Olympic-class swimmer Tracy Caulkins. The school was very accommodating to Tracy's swimming-practice requirements. Had America participated in the 1980 Summer Olympics, she undoubtedly would have won gold or silver medals in her events.

Graduates of Harpeth Hall, almost to a woman, go on to college, earn bachelor's degrees, and quite a few continue on to receive graduate degrees. Harpeth Hall is generally well represented by its graduates in Ivy League colleges and other top universities across the country. According to school headmaster David Wood, Harpeth Hall girls, as a rule, are motivated achievers in life, typically becoming socially active wives of important executives and professionals or professionals themselves.

During her freshman year, Amy's classmates, fewer than one hundred daughters of Nashville's business and professional elite, recognized her charisma and leadership ability and elected her to play the part of George Washington in their annual patriotic class pageant. In her freshman and sophomore years Amy served as maid to the Lady of the Hall, a wholly symbolic honor for the senior girl "who truly embodies the ideals" of the school. She was elected sophomore class president and a junior class representative to the student council. She was also chosen for several honors during her senior year, including class superlative as Most Talented. She was senior class secretary and was often class song leader in all four years. Her crowning glory at Harpeth Hall was her selection as Lady of the Hall the year she was to graduate.

Pat Moran, health and physical education teacher at Harpeth Hall, was the class sponsor for Amy's class of '78. She remembers Amy as an above-average student, low key, well liked, and very involved in class and school activities, such as theater productions.

"She did some theater," recalled Mrs. Moran. "We didn't have the theater department then that we have now, so basically we did a lot of class plays when she was a junior and senior. She did music for it. They always had a class song and she always put the words to it and played the music. She sometimes had a tendency to take on more than she could cope with and she'd get far behind. They'd all do that, and they'd complain, but a lot of it was by choice."

It was at this point, not long after her involvement with the Charismatic group, that Amy took her first tentative steps in the direction that would lead her to the top of the gospel music business in less than eight years. At first, though, Amy was a typically reticent teen who found learning new songs fulfilling, but who had no overweening urge for the spotlight.

"No, no. I was so shy about it," Amy explains. "I sang and wrote songs in my room. It was some cathartic experience. I would sing for the girls at Harpeth Hall. We had our little high school sororities and I'd sing at the slumber parties and gradually I started writing my own songs. I'd kind of interlace my repertoire."

Harpeth Hall provided Amy with her first center-stage experience, just as its predecessor, Ward-Belmont, had earlier provided the club socials and class entertainments at which Sarah Ophelia Colley used her talent to win a niche in that substantially more snobbish atmosphere of Old South wealth and manners. Miss Colley (long since Mrs. Sarah Cannon) began a career at Ward-Belmont that would lead her to become one of the most beloved and long-standing stars of radio's Grand Ole Opry, performing as Miss Minnie Pearl.

Characteristically, Amy's desire to perform for her classmates resulted from two growing motivating forces within her. There was the desire for recognition, which she was fast earning from her classmates for her upbeat leadership qualities, and her desire to express her growing Christian faith. Amy recalls her debut before her first big crowd as an experience with fateful consequences. It established her as a kind of peer minister among her classmates, a lightning rod for many of her young schoolmate's anxieties.

"At Harpeth Hall I had slept through yet another boring

devotional after having become a Christian," she remembered. "For the most part, everybody who got up there was boring. I felt like God was being presented as boring through those devotionals. I went to the headmistress and said, "Could I do a devotional one Wednesday morning?" I had never sung in front of a crowd. I had written one song and I didn't know what I was going to do. I thought, 'I think I'll try to write songs that will tell everybody what I'm feeling.' I learned John Denver, Carole King, James Taylor, songs that everybody knew and were comfortable with to set the atmosphere.

"I think by the time that Wednesday morning rolled around I had written four songs. I planted them in the middle of the rest. It was just thirty minutes. I must have packed ten or twelve songs into that thirty minutes. The juniors and seniors were in the front. The freshmen and sophomores were in the back. I saw people start crying."

That first major performance in Amy's life was cause for some grand anxieties of her own. It also provided a first opportunity for her father to show the kind of support that would become extensive when she later chose music as a career.

"I was very nervous that day at school," Amy says. "But my father and I prayed backstage and when I performed, there wasn't a nervous bone in my body."

If that Harpeth Hall devotional concert marked the beginning of her performing career, it also started something that still happens to her. Her songs generated such emotions in some of her schoolmates that she received a handful of notes from fellow students, not fan mail, but cries for help that would be the first steps in her informal ministry to troubled teens.

"I probably got twelve notes in the next two days. 'What is that you have? Can I get it?' 'I put up such a good front, but I'm wrecked inside.' They were adolescent notes, we were all going through it."

Such trust. Girls her own age and undoubtedly a few who were older began looking to Amy for something big in their lives. As she began leading more school-sponsored sing-alongs, Amy won a special place in the hearts of troubled girls who responded directly to her evangelical exhortations in song. She also earned a growing respect from most of the other students she met. Amy is a person of compelling personal magnetism. In conversation, she makes a person feel as though he or she is the only one in the room. That charisma, paired with her participation in student government, the glee club, and periodic special performances, seemed to hurtle her toward a destiny of sorts. Before the end of her fifteenth year Amy Grant arrived at the threshold of that important life course.

Amy continued writing songs about the things that had meaning for her, for which she knew no other songs to sing. The "Jesus Music" era, the first sustained serious movement toward melding of Christian lyrics and folk, rock, and other nontraditional gospel music forms, had gotten started in the late 1960s. Because it existed largely outside of her earlier religious and social circles, Amy was unaware of most of that music. One wonders if she would have felt so strongly motivated to write her own religious convictions in the musical language of her favorite pop and folksingers if she had been more aware of those early pop and rock gospel pioneers.

The timing of her explosion of talent got her in on the ground floor, with the help of Brown Bannister and Chris Christian. Christian, a graduate of Abilene Christian College, got his first leg up in the Christian music business through Pat Boone. Christian produced the B. J. Thomas album, "Home Where I Belong," which eventually sold more than five hundred thousand copies and earned a gold record to establish the commercial viability of contemporary Christian music, though not necessarily of its gospel-only adherents who lacked the solid pop stardom which

Thomas had already earned. Both Christian and Bannister would become increasingly important figures in the growth of "pop gospel" music.

Amy first befriended, then developed a crush on, Brown Bannister. Bannister was a friend and employee of Christian's as well as a force in the Bible study group that was leading many talented young people to the Belmont Church of Christ, located in what was in the mid-seventies a seedy section of Nashville's Music Row area. The section of famed Sixteenth Avenue South where the Belmont Church is located was a well-to-do residential section of downtown Nashville in its heyday. The substantial homes there had been built after the Civil War along what was once the two-mile-long driveway from the outskirts of downtown Nashville to the Belmont Mansion—where famed political hostess Adelica Acklen held court with Union officers, many decades before it became the Ward-Belmont School. Those days were long gone when the first studios and publishing companies began to take advantage of the declining property prices to locate on Sixteenth Avenue. Across the street from the church building is the Koinonia bookstore and coffeehouse, which continues to be an important gathering place for Charismatic musical ministry.

Brown Bannister, many years her senior, took the somewhat smitten Amy Grant under his wing. She began hanging around the recording studio where Bannister worked. In the most time-honored traditions of music-business apprenticeship, she swept floors and demagnetized tape heads for the privilege of watching how recordings were made. Bannister not only let her hang around the studio to learn about making recordings, but complimented her songs and encouraged her musical interests. It was Bannister who helped her music reach the right ears in the first place, leading to Amy's recording contract with Word Records.

Amy's burgeoning creativity produced more new songs

and after a while she decided to put them down on tape for her parents, if not posterity. Despite her dreams of singing professionally when she got older, Amy at fifteen did not realize how good her plaintive, teenaged folk-gospel compositions were. Her high school performances didn't always reflect a tremendous amount of preparation, which indicated she had no particular burning drive to become a recording star and professional performer.

"After a while I just made a tape of my songs for my parents," Amy explained. "I thought, 'I can't write this down, I can't read music. If I don't record them nobody's going to remember these wonderful hit songs.' That tape caused me so much embarrassment because every time somebody came over to our house our father and mother would say, 'Come listen to this tape little Amy did.' Then, without my knowing it, somebody took this tape and called a record company in Texas and said, 'We've got a girl here in Nashville who sings.' So when I was called to do an album I thought it was a practical joke. I had never sung at any kind of ticketed affair. I had always sung at my high school and I did a concert at MBA [Montgomery Bell Academy—an exclusive boys prep school nearby] . . ."

That somebody who played Amy's rough tape for the bigwigs at Word Records was Chris Christian. He had only recently entered into a deal with the Texas-based music company to find and develop new Christian artists from among the ripening crop of youthful singer/songwriters he had seen at Koinonia. The story of how he first heard Amy Grant's tape is one of those peculiar happenstances that some people call fate.

Chapter 4

It's strange how important connections are sometimes made through the most seemingly insignificant occurrences. Many musicians and would-be artists spend years plodding along in their craft, just hoping that someday they'll be tapped on the shoulder in one of those star-crossed incidents that turns travail into triumph. Some people call it luck, others ascribe it to the mysterious direction of an unseen hand, but there's no substitute in the music business for being in the right place at the right time with the right stuff.

Amy went to Brown Bannister to ask a favor. Would he please run a copy of her rough demonstration tape off at the studio for her? No problem, he said. And who should be hanging around the sound room when the tape was being copied but the newly hired Word Records representative, Chris Christian.

Unbeknownst to her, Christian took a copy of Amy's tape for his bosses at Word. He was so taken with her voice and material that he couldn't wait for the U.S. Postal Service to deliver the tape to Waco, Texas—he called them and played the tape over the phone. They responded positively on the spot. Mike Blanton, then head of the fledgling Nashville office for Word Records, was impressed as well. Though

Word's Nashville office was new and small, Word Inc. was probably the biggest gospel record company in the nation. It became a subsidiary of the American Broadcasting Company (parent company of the ABC television network) in 1974, giving Word an even greater bank of capital to call upon to expand its operations. Word Inc. is now a $50 million-plus subsidiary of Capital Cities Communications Corporation, which acquired ABC in 1984.

While Amy was setting gospel music professionals on their ears with her compelling music, she in no way considered herself solely a gospel songwriter. Amy was doing her own thing within her own local framework of friends and classmates, blithely unaware that she was being scouted by one of the biggest and most powerful gospel music companies in the business. Her ignorance of the gospel music industry was such that had she known Word Records was scouting her, she would not have known whether that was a big deal or not. She was writing her Christian-message songs for herself and her friends.

"That's what I wrote, not because it was the only thing I wanted to sing, but because it was the only thing I didn't have songs for," she says. "By the time I'd written a dozen songs, that was what those dozen songs were about. So, a Christian record company heard my tape over the phone, called me up, and said, 'We want you to do a Christian album.' I've never stopped loving the old pop music stuff, but suddenly people said, 'You have a knack for expressing this.' Because they offered me an opportunity to sing that, I did."

This last statement is one of the keys to understanding Amy Grant's natural progression to her summer 1985 plunge into the pop music charts. It also goes a long way toward explaining Amy's uniquely contradictory position in professional gospel music circles. She is heralded by the media as the "queen of gospel music," yet for all her GMA Dove Awards and Grammys, Amy's career has achieved its

Singing makes Amy Grant happier than just about anything.
Photo by Neil Pond—Courtesy of *Music City News.*

Amy Grant (bottom, left) was active in the President's Council, a leadership group at Harpeth Hall.

Holding class office had its lighter moments, as Amy (top, left) and other class presidents hammed it up for the camera as the 1975–76 school year got under way at Harpeth Hall.

Amy's senior class portrait.

Amy (standing second from right with other class officers) was
elected president of her sophomore class in high school.

As a junior, Amy was a court member to Lady of the Hall, the next year, students noted: "Amy is most well-known throughout the school as a person with a singular talent for singing and for living as she sings: with love and laughter."

Amy and a classmate perform a duet during the school's annual arts festival.   Photos courtesy of Harpeth Hall School

Amy Grant—sophomore class photo.

This heart-shaped balloon held over Amy's head by friends showed the respect and affection in which classmates held the budding Christian singer.   Photos courtesy of Harpeth Hall School

The yellow brick edifice of Belmont Church is home of the Charismatic congregation that Amy found in her teenage search for herself and God.

Photo by Bob Millard

A bouquet of magnolia blossoms accented Amy's flowing dress as she posed with two little attendants as her school bestowed upon her the highest honor to a graduating senior by naming her Lady of the Hall.   Photo courtesy of Harpeth Hall School

Located in what was a large home on once-fashionable Sixteenth Avenue South, Koinonia coffeehouse/bookstore has been a center for contemporary Christian songwriters like Amy Grant and Gary Chapman.   Photo by Bob Millard

greatest gains by going outside traditional gospel music industry channels.

In order to gain a better understanding of Amy Grant as a contemporary Christian superstar—and why her tremendous success is such a unique phenomenon—it helps to know a little bit about the development of gospel music and its relatively recent subclassification: contemporary Christian music.

One can find its roots as far back as the early days of colonial America, after the Pilgrims, here in large part for religious freedom, settled on the northeast coast of the New World. The Protestant religion the Puritans brought and refined here had no stimulating music to ameliorate the effects of the long, droning, and arid sermons of their clergy. In 1740, a British evangelist named George Whitefield sailed to New England and held the New World's first revival.

Whitefield unleashed a tirade of enthusiasm and fervor never before seen on these shores. He preached a personal salvation based on a deep conversion experience, which found many converts here, introducing an element of emotionalism that has run in deep veins through many American religious movements from that time on. Whitefield started a movement that generated a vast body of new church music in his time, and he set in motion the forces of emotional release through religion that would culminate in modern gospel music at its finest.

The early 1800s saw a new wave of Christian revivalism sweeping the frontier states of the newly established nation. Kentucky is said by some to have hosted the first frontier "camp meetings." Bonfires lit the sky while barely educated preachers shouted sweet salvation and its alternative of fire and brimstone to frontier communities at rousing evening meetings. Folk music forms, derived mainly from Scottish and English tunes, combined with rough and ragged pioneer enthusiasm as hymns were raised and the camp-song genre was born.

The main foundations of the traditional gospel music industry developed in the South. Coming together over the course of a few hundred years, gospel music, both black and white varieties, stemmed from the basic four-part harmony form and shared a message of faith in a living God. To be certain, there were and still are important differences between the two. It is doubtful, for example, that middle-class whites, who never experienced the chains of slavery and oppression, could have fully understood the passionate themes of the sorrows of this world and the ringing call for freedom in the "better world to come" that run through black spiritual music.

First to carry the heritage of slave spirituals to national and eventual international note were the Jubilee Singers from Fisk University, founded in Nashville immediately following the Civil War. Fisk was a financially strapped institution when its newly established eleven-member Jubilee Singers hit the road to sing traditional black spirituals in churches and auditoriums for the privilege of taking up an offering afterward. The survival of Fisk today is a legacy of the appeal of their gospel sounds. Within a year they had established themselves as one of the most moving experiences in religious music anywhere in the world, drawing tears from England's Queen Victoria when the monarch heard them perform in 1872. Famed abolitionist Henry Ward Beecher described some of their music as "wild slave songs, some of which seem like the inarticulate wails of breaking hearts made dumb by slavery." It was actually considerably more anglicized than that, but the sounds and feelings were new to the staid Northern antislavery propagandist.

Early progenitors of modern black gospel music included Thomas A. Dorsey, Clara Ward, and Mahalia Jackson, children of the early twentieth century. Dorsey and

Jackson found themselves in Chicago during the 1920s and 1930s when black gospel began to push aside the more anglicized choral forms of official black church music in the hearts of men and women, coalescing from old spiritual, blues, and newer jazz influences. Dorsey took the pure rhythm of spiritual/blues forms and injected it with gospel messages, eventually making his mark with choral arrangements that formed the backbone of a lot of white gospel favorites. He skated between the secular ranks of "race music," writing hits for blues star Ma Rainey, and ecstatic gospel forms until he switched to gospel solely in 1929. Early in his career, he was roundly criticized by conservative church circles, just as Amy has been, for mixing the Lord's word with "the devil's music."

So influential was Dorsey as a songwriter and musical force that Viv Broughton, a historian of black gospel music, said of him, "More than any other individual, Thomas A. Dorsey is gospel and his story is the story of gospel." His songs became standards in both white and black gospel music. Mahalia Jackson toured with Dorsey for a time, singing both his ballads and his rousing, blues-filtered gospel shouting songs, and selling sheet music for a dime a tune. Together and later separately their fame and influence spread across all boundaries. Mahalia became the first superstar of black gospel music.

Some of the pioneering traditional white gospel family acts from the 1920s and 1930s continue their traditions today. Their music is grouped as a commercial category under the title Traditional Music. Family groups such as the LeFevres, the Chuck Wagon Gang, the Singing Speer Family, the Thrasher Family, and the Stamps Quartet were on a circuit that encompassed most of the Old South, Texas, Oklahoma, and the Southern states of the Eastern Seaboard. By the end of World War II black and white gospel music were firmly established in that region and ready to expand. Families from the South migrated to the industrial

centers of the northern Midwest and to other economic
opportunities on the West Coast, taking their religions and
musical tastes with them. The above-mentioned musical
acts have few, if any, original members still performing with
them, but all continue to make records and tour in concert
(though the Thrashers have left gospel to "go country").

Women in the traditional white gospel acts often provided the focus for the group, though they never went out
on their own to become soloists. Eva May LeFevre, Vestal
Goodman, and Lena "Mom" Speer were strong vocal features of their respective family gospel groups from the late
twenties, in some cases, through the fifties in others. Sisters
Rose Karnes and Anna Gordon were the most important
vocal members of the Chuck Wagon Gang for many years.
It was not until a few years before Amy Grant entered the
picture that women really emerged as solo stars in the
religious music field.

White Pentecostalism, a radical Protestant religious
practice of the poorer classes, and many black Christian
denominations have a common trait: explosive emotionalism. Many separate stylistic elements of black and white
gospel music, as developed in the 1940s, have been combined in today's gospel genres. From raucous "holy roll-
ers" to the most retiring, off-key "cracker" quartets, gospel
singers addressed working people's hopes and fears, their
joy and sadness, dreams and their need for acceptable emotional outlets. Participation in an all-day sing on the
grounds of rural Primitive Baptist church or a stomping-
good concert by a gospel group in the heart of Detroit
could send the old, the lonely, the wage-slave and the pe-
rennial underdog of America's agricultural and industrial
centers home renewed, refreshed, and ready to face the
challenge and harshness of their individual day-to-day realities.

There were groups such as the Blackwood Brothers, the
Stamps, the Rebels, the Speer Family, and the Statesmen

whose enormous personal magnetism gave their gospel performances tremendous cathartic effect on their audiences. The Statesmen, in particular, were precursors of the outrageous and energetic stage antics of the early rock performers. They earned the label "sensational," drawing a headline in *The Saturday Evening Post* in the fifties to the effect that "They Put Rhythm in Religion."

"They did such fantastic arrangements and were so smooth, it was just unreal," said GMA's Don Butler, himself a working gospel singer of the era. "They caused the excitement. Hovie Lister, a longtime member of the Masters V, would shake his hair down on the stage. His hair was very curly, though he wore it pomaded in the 'wet-look' style of the day, and he would shake it loose and it would get all frizzy on stage. They would jump up on the piano and jump up on the piano stool to jump off the stage into the audience and all these things."

Clearly, rock and roll borrowed some very important elements of gospel music. Certain early sounds of white rockabilly and boogie-woogie had slipped into Pentecostal music of the deep South in the late forties. It may be surprising for some people to learn that cousins Jerry Lee Lewis, Mickey Gilley, and evangelist Jimmy Swaggart learned to play piano in the same Louisiana backwoods Pentecostal church. They were undoubtedly influenced heavily by the regional powerhouse act that reached prominence in the early 1940s, the Stamps.

"Back in the forties the Stamps Quartet [was] under the leadership of Virgil O. Stamps, who was the dean of bass singers," recalled Butler. "He went on KRLD radio, which was a 50,000-watt clear-channel station in Dallas, Texas. He had programs that reached out into all areas, then he went on to a Del Rio, Texas station."

V. O. Stamps was being heard even beyond the borders of this country then and his style of music began to be identified as *the* white gospel sound of the time. Stamps was a man of sufficient commercial sensibilities and moved to make the most of this.

"He was promoter and a hustler if I ever saw one in my life," Butler said with a smile. "He had a magic touch, he knew what would work, and he would put it to work. He teamed up with his crew and established a school in Texas where all these guys and gals could come and study shape-note music and quartet singing."

He also founded a publishing enterprise called the Stamps-Baxter Music and Printing Company to publish songbooks of tunes for vocal groups. He disseminated his style of music by sponsoring quartets and helping them get on radio in cities with 50,000-watt stations, primarily in the strongholds of traditional gospel music—just about any-where below the Mason-Dixon line. The acts performed on radio and worked concerts, selling tremendous amounts of Stamps-Baxter songbooks, the most widely marketed form of gospel music. Among groups performing during that period in conjunction with Stamps's enterprises were the Speer Family and the Blackwood Brothers. All-night sings, one of the most popular forums for traditional Southern gospel music through the 1960s, grew out of a major show which marked the closing of the Stamps school.

The numerous, constantly touring Vaughn Quartets were also vehicles for songbook sales. In addition, the Vaughn publishing organization pioneered gospel radio broadcasting in Tennessee. Blind Andy Jenkins ("God Gave Noah the Rainbow Sign") and his family did the same for Georgia.

In the late 1950s, black "soul music" began to creep onto white pop radio stations, and gospel singers such as Sam Cooke and Aretha Franklin "went over" to commercial soul singing. Cooke and Franklin both came from family acts in the Spiritual traditions of commercial gospel music. The term Spiritual is still used, primarily as a euphemism for a variety of black gospel forms. There are subspecies of Spiritual gospel music, such as traditional and contemporary. Cooke originally sang with the Singing Children and Highway HQ, groups that featured two of his sisters and a brother. Aretha Franklin was touted as a prodigy from age twelve, when she sang her first solo in the church where her father preached. He made preaching records and often traveled as a dynamic preacher with gospel caravans.

Amy Grant's easy slide into out-and-out pop songs in 1985 may have come from sharing this thought from the late Sam Cooke: "I was happy enough on the gospel trail . . . but the more I thought about the pop field, the more interesting it became." By 1960, at the peak of the soul music trend, record men looked at black churches for the potential of "black gold," which seemed inexhaustible and there for the taking.

Sadly, unless they took extraordinary pains to retain their close connections with their gospel following, black gospel singers were spurned by their old gospel fans after they made the switch to pop. Aretha Franklin avoided this fate by constantly reaffirming her gospel roots. Sam Cooke was booed off stage when he tried to make guest appearances on the gospel circuit. Therein lies a danger that may face gospel acts even today. One big plus for Amy Grant's pop/gospel ambivalence is that it attracts a young, nonfundamentalist audience for whom secular pop music is already an acceptable form of expression.

Back in the late fifties and early sixties, it was difficult to return once you stepped outside the Lord's music. After they became Elvis Presley's first backup group, the Jordanaires quartet was never again embraced by the gospel world. In a later era, the Imperials and J. D. Sumner and the Stamps were applauded for their work as Elvis Presley's backup groups because they were seen as bringing Presley into the gospel fold rather than abandoning their own roots.

B. J. Thomas provided the most graphic example of gospel fans' recent inability to fully accept mainstream gospel mixing with mainstream pop music. In the mid-seventies Thomas began to mix his contemporary Christian career with his pop hits. He found his concerts became a war zone inhabited in part by hard-core Christian fans who booed his secular hits like "Raindrops Keep Falling on My Head" and secular fans who were at very least uncomfortable with his stageside confessions of faith. Thomas was attempting to leave behind a severe drug problem and rebuild a marriage that nearly expired from his own raging abuses. He was as true a prodigal son as any pop-singer convert had ever been, but there was little sympathy within his Christian community for the complexities of his life and career.

"In his case," said GMA spokesman Butler, "the Christians did what they are known to do—they shoot their wounded. It's a shame."

The father of the middle-of-the-road, adult-oriented, pop-gospel music now known as Inspirational gospel is Ralph Carmichael. Amy usually skates the outer fringes of this form. Carmichael was a conductor-arranger for pop acts like Lena Horne, Nat King Cole, and others in the fifties. Carmichael started adding pop string and brass arrangements to gospel lyrics in the 1950s. Thurlow Spurr was a student at ultrafundamentalist church college Bob Jones University when Carmichael released his first pop-orchestrated gospel albums. Spurr was nearly thrown out of school for smuggling Ralph Carmichael's pop-sound gospel records on campus and playing them in his room. Cam Floria and Thurlow Spurr got together with Carmichael to form the Continental Singers, eventually going out on their own.

The early sixties saw middle-of-the-road, pop-style music coming into its own in a legitimate form of Christian-aimed entertainment. Men like Thurlow Spurr and Cam Floria, whose musical roots were the West Coast pop sound rather than the four-part harmonies of the Southeast, formed squeaky-clean ensembles of enthusiastic teens and young adults to tour the country singing songs reflecting positive middle-class philosophy and uplifting Christian gospel messages. Spurr's Spurlows and Floria's Continentals toured several ensembles at one time under the same names. They combined the more socially acceptable elements of current pop music with gospel-oriented lyrics, steering well clear of the more gyrating gris-gris rhythms of rock. What's more, they updated their music periodically to reflect the evolution of pop styles.

In 1964 the Catholic Church helped blaze a new musical trail by adapting contemporary music forms to Christian uses, accepting a folk mass for use in its worship service, Ray Repp's *Mass for Young Americans*. These folk masses and Protestant services were quite the vogue during the mid-sixties, paralleling the "hootenanny" folk music revival that swept the nation in the wake of the Civil Rights Movement.

Country music has traditionally had a strong gospel music element. The Grand Ole Opry still manages to feature a gospel tune in nearly every fifteen-minute segment of its Friday and Saturday night shows. One of the first acts to come from gospel roots to major mainstream commercial country music in modern times was the Statler Brothers. This regional quartet, based in Virginia, broke big after joining Johnny Cash as a backup vocal group in the early 1960s. In 1966 the Statler Brothers topped the Beatles with a Grammy win with the deceptively simple, but plain American poetic genius of the Lew DeWitt tune "Flowers on the Wall."

Other gospel quartets made bids for mainstream acceptance after their success. The biggest gospel act to make the turn successfully was a forty-year-old group that was originally formed in Knoxville as the Country Cut-ups. They often entertained the religious of a small East Tennessee community that in the early 1940s began to swarm with researchers and military personnel working in stifling secrecy on the development of the nation's first atomic weapons. Taking the name the Oak Ridge Boys in the early 1950s, the group went through numerous changes in personnel before the Country Music Association legitimized their country standing by naming them the 1978 Vocal Group of the Year. Megahits such as the remake of Dallas Frazier's "Elvira" and an equally contagious sing-along number, "Bobbie Sue," carried them into the pantheon of country music demigods. As country music experienced a mid-eighties retrenchment following the so-called "Urban Cowboy" popularity of 1979–82, the Oak Ridge Boys continued to be one of the category's top concert draws. They are one of the few true superstar acts in the mid-eighties country-entertainment business, along with Kenny Rogers, Dolly Parton, Alabama, and Willie Nelson.

Also achieving some notoriety as gospel-gone-country acts are the Thrasher Brothers, the Four Guys, and, especially noteworthy for her sale figures, Cristy Lane. During the 1970s, Cristy Lane enjoyed a fairly lackluster career as a country singer, having been one of many country hopefuls who occasionally paid the bills by undertaking small-scale tours of entertainment-starved fire bases in Vietnam. Her personal life had been marked by the tragedy of her husband/manager Lee Stoller's minor criminal conviction and subsequent brief imprisonment in the late seventies. All that changed when Cristy earned her first (and only) Number One country hit in the early eighties with a sing-song inspirational tune, "One Day at a Time," based on the pledge/prayer of Alcoholics Anonymous.

Cristy Lane, a pleasant woman of modest voice and beauty, struck a chord with that song as the average working "Everywoman." Her life would later become grist for a successful mail-order biography named for her biggest hit. Whatever his other attributes, Lee Stoller proved himself a master at television marketing, turning "One Day at a Time" into a reported two-million-selling album. She has probably tallied four million album sales to date, though RIAA does not certify sales that are not reported through auditable retail outlets. As a country artist, Cristy joined country anomalies Slim Whitman and Boxcar Willie as an act whose records move in massive quantities through channels and by methods that fall outside official industry charts. Within the religious music camp, she is firmly in the Inspirational column.

Contemporary Christian music, as a category with multiple forms, really got started among Christian youth in the late sixties. As a youth-oriented rock form that alienated adults as much as most secular rock sounds did, contemporary Christian sounds got started as part of "the generation gap."

Assessing the sociological ramifications of the late 1960s in general terms, drugs, hard rock and psychedelic music, alternative religions and life-styles began to characterize what *Time* and other magazines by 1967 were calling "the Youth Culture." Opposition to the Vietnam War and the revolution in pop music wrought by such musical pacesetters as the Beatles and Bob Dylan helped change the perceptions of young Americans about many things. There were important changes in young people's demands on religion.

Church attendance by young people fell off radically in the late 1960s and early 1970s. For some, such movements as Youth for Christ and Campus Crusades for Christ brought a more intense and personal form of Christianity to fill their needs. Others, especially those who were being ground up and spit out by the street culture in California's "hippie" enclaves, found their spiritual homes in street ministries that preached with a charismatic fervor. These street ministries often included coffeehouse forums at which converts would sing to each other about their new-found relationship with God.

George Whitefield would have approved heartily of the

whole scene. As oblivious to these developments as the fourteen-year-old Amy Grant was when she began plucking out her first painfully awkward guitar chords, she nevertheless entered an important new tributary of the contemporary Christian music stream when she found a spiritual home that included Nashville's Koinonia coffeehouse/bookstore.

"I knew [contemporary Christian music] existed because I'd always heard some gospel music," says Amy. "I didn't know the name of one group. By the time I was in junior high school I knew of André Crouch, but I didn't have any gospel records. In fact, the only group I even liked was a local group called Dogwood."

Contemporary Christian singers and songwriters found compatible spiritual and creative homes on such gospel labels as Milk & Honey, Lion & Lamb, Maranatha! Records, Word, and the Benson Company family of labels, but it was often difficult to get their records distributed outside their immediate vicinity. There was little placement of Christian records for teens in Bible and Sunday School book outlets, unlike today. Hard rock contemporary Christian music existed primarily within a sort of Christian underground in those years. Most churches objected to the rock medium for the gospel message, and secular record distributors and outlets usually had no idea what to do with it, so they did nothing.

Capitol Records, which distributed the Beatles' records through the sixties, issued one of the very first gospel rock albums by an artist whose sole intention was to broadcast and propagate his faith. That artist was Larry Norman. Norman left a successful pop group called People after a song called "I Love You (But the Words Won't Come)" reached the Top 15 on pop charts. Norman's Christian followup was nowhere near as commercially successful for Capitol, who later pawned the record off on the Nashville-based Benson Company. Norman was the target of large-scale scorn and protest from establishment churches, whose youth ministries provided the mainstay of the contemporary Christian concert circuit outside of California.

Another secular artist, folk-rocker Barry McGuire, whose hit "Eve of Destruction" topped the pop charts in 1965, bottomed out of the secular music industry after bouts with drugs and depression and became a "born again" Christian. He turned his musical talents to expressing his newfound faith, using the same kinds of raw and rocking styles that marked his secular music. The "generation gap" of those turbulent times hit these gospel rockers twice as hard as it did secular rock artists because McGuire, Norman, and others addressed a subject close to the hearts of fundamentalist Christian adults with music they didn't like and couldn't fully appreciate.

Yet, Norman, McGuire, and others were heard. Their music reached young people hungry for the gospel message set to a music that didn't sound like a funeral dirge. Their lyrics spoke to teens and young adults in their own language.

"Larry Norman and Barry McGuire were considered weirdos because their lyrics were so off the wall as far as traditional gospel music people were concerned," Butler explains. "It certainly caught a lot of attention."

The gospel rock underground grew through the midseventies as an important communicating tool for what was called the Jesus People movement. Other significant movements in contemporary Christian music of those times included equally controversial, but usually more profitable, developments in musical theater. Plays with biblical premises began to proliferate rapidly following the stupendous success of Andrew Lloyd Webber/Tim Rice-penned scores for "Joseph and the Amazing Technicolor Dreamcoat" (1967–68) and "Jesus Christ Superstar" (1971–73). Neither Webber nor Rice was at the time a deeply committed Christian writer, but Christian themes were dramatically legitimized through the genre of musical theater by their works. The notoriety and success of these and other plays took the Jesus movement to secular audiences in such a way as to help spread and strengthen the movements sometimes known as Charismatic and born again Christianity, both attracting more and more young people.

The slow growth of Charismatic youth ministries and consumer support of contemporary Christian music paralleled each other. Because gospel music's splintered commercial categories are, taken separately, still relatively small and divided commercial sectors of the record business, *Billboard* magazine features alternating bi-weekly gospel charts for the separate Inspirational and Spiritual categories, based on retail store reports rather than on air play. Subcategories within these two groups include contemporary, worship, praise, and traditional forms. Mixing pop and rock music to bridge the gap between Middle of the Road (MOR) Inspirational and hard-rock contemporary Christian sounds, Amy Grant has benefitted from the years of effort spent by contemporary Christian artists—most of whom never tasted much commercial success—trying to overcome active resistance by churches.

Don Butler pinpoints Amy Grant's entry into contemporary music and rise to the top of its sales charts this way: "Amy Grant as a young person rode the crest that started in the sixties with the 'Jesus People' movement. Some people called them Jesus freaks but what it consisted of was that generation which was born and bred on the Beatles era of pop music."

Amy, as a solo white female gospel star, followed such trailblazers as Evie Tornquist, Cynthia Clawson, and Reba Rambo, some of the first women to emerge in the late seventies who went solo and became stars. All had at least one thing in common—they were all well known in church music or mainstream gospel music circles before emerging as solo artists. Amy was different in that respect.

Though the Lord is a component of her music—if not always by name then in important attitudes and circumstances—Amy is an outsider to the gospel industry. She does not come from the gospel-singing family traditions of Southern gospel music, nor has she sought much exposure at the churches where gospel acts traditionally found their audience, their inspiration, and their limits. One also senses a different sort of commitment to her career as a gospel singer that certainly separates her from the other women in gospel music. She has indicated that if her singing career ever takes a nosedive or ceases to be fun, "I'll go home and have babies because I'm singing to the same kids over and over again and it's just not worth it to my marriage, not worth it to my own life."

Amy Grant has been castigated by the fundamentalists, as have all contemporary and some Inspirational singers, without suffering either career setbacks or the mental anguish of a forced apostasy. Her gospel message, while not strong enough for hard-core gospel advocates, did not interfere with her assimilation into the pop mainstream. She regards her positive message music as an undiluted representation of her religious orientation. Because her way of singing her faith has been so new and different, yet so incredibly successful, she has often been discussed more in terms of who she is *not,* rather than who she is. She has made her mark by ignoring many of the time-tested traditions of gospel music and its industry. Had she gone those old ways, she would never have earned her shot at the pop field, nor would some veins of gospel music have seen the popularity they enjoy today.

Chapter 5

When Amy Grant began her recording career at age sixteen, she was as much a product of the religious trends of her adolescent years as of the musical movement she encountered. As the elements of worship got further and further afield from traditional Church of Christ doctrine, it was Amy Grant who knowingly led in an important final step in separating the Belmont Church from its mother church.

"Amy was writing these songs and sang one of them at church," Finto remembers fondly. "We were a noninstrumental Church of Christ but she sang one of them at church with her guitar, which really sort of broke the barrier to the instrumental music here. That was something that we then had to deal with, but our elders as a whole didn't have any strong convictions against instrumental music. Why not use it since we had so many musicians here? We had so many gifted people who could play all over but they couldn't play in their own home church."

The Belmont Church under Don Finto's leadership has been a church in evolution. One of the decisive steps in that evolutionary process, in relation to Amy Grant's Christian singing and songwriting career, was the church's establishment of the Koinonia bookstore and coffeehouse in a store-front next door to the sanctuary.

With a strong sense of social outreach, this place for musical ministry became a focus for local youths and others whose musical interests were beginning to be expressed there. It became a small but important place for the touring folk and rock acts of succeeding eras of contemporary Christian music. With the opening of Koinonia coffee-house, the Belmont Church took a step that would rival the seminal contributions of Calvary Chapel, in Costa Mesa, California, where the Jesus Movement got its institutional beginnings in the sixties and where Maranatha! Records artists started one of the nation's first centers of youth-generated Jesus rock music.

"Through some money that a friend gave to one of our brothers, Jim Bevis, who was an associate minister here then, we started a bookstore and coffeehouse ministry," Finto explains. "It was the kind of place where people came in with their guitars and sat around and sang together around tables and had tea, cokes, and cookies, coffee. We had it every Saturday night, sometimes even Friday nights. Sometimes there would be maybe twenty or twenty-five people there. Sometimes fifteen people, sometimes maybe forty people. It was really a small coffeehouse ministry."

Big birds hatch from small eggs, and the growth of Nash-ville as an important center for contemporary Christian music was originally focused on Koinonia. Early contempo-rary Christian, rock-flavored bands headquartering at Koi-nonia included Dogwood and Homecoming, the latter fea-turing Brown Bannister.

From age fifteen to seventeen, Amy Grant played at her school and occasionally at Koinonia. As with her Harpeth Hall performances, these were informal events for her, epi-sodes that provided little if any of the kind of real live concert experience she began gaining after her first record came out. When she was sixteen, Amy was brought before the studio microphone to record by Brown Bannister and Chris Christian.

Amy's first album, titled simply "Amy Grant," was recorded in Nashville. Confidence and experience have since led her to Colorado's Caribou Ranch recording center, where Elton John, Nitty Gritty Dirt Band, and other mainstream rock acts have cut records, but confidence was the missing element when she was first signed by Word. Bannister got Amy to relax for the recording session by turning out all the lights in the studio. Letting Amy sing in total darkness, where no one could see the apprehension in her face or observe her wincing at mistakes, was the only way Bannister could get her through those sessions. Amy laughs now about her first recording experience.

"When I was seventeen I was just an idiot, so naive . . . I was a total moron," Amy says in assessment of that first recording project. "I was too embarrassed to sing with the lights on."

That album, atrocious cover and all, sold more than fifty thousand copies. While that is certainly modest by pop standards, it was at that time a resounding gospel success, and even today would place her in the sales league of one of the most articulate and talented contemporary Christian cult artists, Mark Heard.

According to Don Butler, there had already been a groundbreaker who had changed career emphasis and left a perfect hole for Amy to fill in the contemporary Christian market.

"You have to remember that at that time Word's big candy stick was Evie Tornquist," Butler explains. "She had that wholesome pixie look, those cute eyes. She took the country by storm and probably sold more records than any other gospel artist at that time.

"Amy was not middle-of-the-road and cutesy like Evie. She had a hard, driving beat [unlike Evie], but with acceptable lyrics [like Evie]. She was not an instant hit. Her music was quite a bit softer on those first records than it is now. You have to remember that Amy Grant has only been a 'star' since about [the middle of 1983]. They had her out at Opryland Hotel early in the morning singing for the Madison [Tennessee] Chamber of Commerce breakfast as recently as that, which she certainly doesn't have to do now.

"Evie Tornquist was changing her style and then she fell in love with Pele Karlsson, who was more interested in the ministry. It was felt in most circles that he influenced her to get involved more in the ministry aspect. Evie lost her position as the darling of gospel music because she curtailed her travel, changed her style of music and her emphasis [from entertaining to ministry]."

Amy was seventeen, and already quite popular at Harpeth Hall for her outgoing friendliness. She became the subject of peer adulation for a few weeks when the album first came out. Her high school yearbook for 1977–78 reported the phenomenon this way: "Amy's first album came out during the school year and for a week or so many girls carried a copy of the album with their books, waiting for a chance to get her to sign it. The album seemed to many to be the fruit of the years of Amy's concerts on the lawn and in the auditorium, her leadership of club and class sings, and most of all her successful attempt to live in a way consistent with her joyful and uplifting songs."

As witnessed by that account, Amy was being put on a pedestal from a very early stage in her career. Partly from self-conscious modesty, Amy prefers not to be seen by her fans as somebody bigger than life, someone whose life is any holier or happier than anybody else's. One of her most endearing messages to her younger fans is that no one is perfect. Amy told a television interviewer the following story to illustrate her own teenaged curiosity about worldly temptations.

"But by the time senior year rolled around, I don't think I had changed that much," Amy says. "I had a big blowout senior year. I got as drunk as the girl sitting next to me. It's the only time I got really snockered. There were forty-eight of us girls in London [as part of the Harpeth Hall Winterim travel and education program]. We all got sick and had a two-hour ride on the bus the next day. A girl said, 'Everybody was so sick and you were sitting on the front row of the bus praying, "I'm really sorry I blew it this time." ' That happening opened up doors to talk to so many more people about God. It showed me that even when I totally flopped, something good came out of it. That something in that case was three different girls became Christians and their lives obviously changed. They were very vocal about it in different ways."

Amy was on her way, yet she was barely aware of the building momentum that would sweep her into the hot spotlight of stardom in a few short years' time.

Chapter 6

For several years after Amy Grant signed her contract with Word Records, her musical universe remained manageably small and close to home. The support she got from her friends at Harpeth Hall, from her adoring family, and from the growing circle of Koinonia coffeehouse regulars was gratifying to the young singer/songwriter. Her composing talent seemed to grow with each new song she added to her repertoire. For Amy, despite the record deal, these small-scale, local performances were all a pleasant and familiar game. She had no special drive to become a gospel music superstar and consequently had developed little knowledge of professional entertaining.

Amy entered her career rather naively. There was some confusion in her mind when she was told that she could do her first concert for $300. Not realizing that her hosts would pay *her* for the privilege, rather than the other way around, Amy protested. "I only have $500 in my savings and I need it," she said.

Her show in those days was simple and low key. She sat on a stool, holding her guitar, and shared a few stories and songs. She had no burning ambition to become a big-time entertainer. In fact, she often told people during her late teen years that she wanted nothing better than to go to college then find a husband and raise a family. At seventeen, she was about to be catapulted out of her comfortable local and family setting into a growing limelight for which she was neither personally nor professionally prepared.

From the time Word Records signed the high school sophomore until they finally released her first record, "Amy Grant," in 1977, the protective environment of family at home and friends at Koinonia and Harpeth Hall helped Amy to grow musically. Her lights-out recording wasn't done in one of Nashville's many state-of-the-art studios where country artists made their hit records. Only two short blocks away from Amy's Belmont Church is RCA's famed Studio B where Elvis Presley and Jim Reeves had cut many of their early hits. Even closer is historic Columbia Studio B where Owen Bradley made fabulous Brenda Lee hits like "I'm Sorry" and "Rockin' Around the Christmas Tree" and Billy Sherrill produced heart-wrenching George Jones and Tammy Wynette records. Amy's vinyl debut was recorded in a small in-home studio that featured plumbing as an unpredictable special effect.

"The first album was made in a basement studio," Amy recalls with a laugh. "And every time someone flushed the toilet upstairs, we had to redo the song."

The basement was in Chris Christian's house near Brentwood, Tennessee, a pricey suburban community south of the city. He called it the Gold Mine studio and, true to its name, its ad hoc design resembled some strange underground cavern. When Amy was cutting there with Christian and Bannister during her last year in high school, most normal-sized people had to stoop to enter it. The ceiling was cluttered with architectural necessities so that it was impossible to stand up in a certain part of the control room.

Musicians who played on that first album included Ron Elder, Steve Chapman, and Bannister. All were members of Pastor Don Finto's growing music ministry at Belmont Church and players with Nashville's premier Christian rock

Amy Grant cracked the books at Vanderbilt University, but her travel schedule still kept her from graduating when she flunked several mandatory-attendance courses. Photo by Georgia Nell Dukes

Amy joked that most of her college classmates knew her only as
"the girl who asked a lot of dumb questions," even though she
was fast becoming the biggest single star in gospel music.

Photo by Georgia Nell Dukes

Gary Chapman jumps for joy in 1981 when he is named the Gospel Music Association's Songwriter of the Year. The billboard behind him tells all of Nashville about his accomplishment.

Photo by Chip Schofield

In Concert—Amy winds up . . .

Photos by John McCormick

then lets go of an emotional note.

As she sings an early hit song, Amy definitely has her "Father's Eyes."

Photo by Owen Cartwright

This was the moment Gary Chapman had been working toward for three years, as he made Amy his wife in an early summer wedding in 1982. They went to Canada for a quick honeymoon but Mr. and Mrs. Gary Chapman would take a five-week, second-honeymoon/concert tour of Europe only a few weeks later.

Photo by Owen Cartwright

"Did you ever see such a thing?" Amy asks friend Melinda Scruggs as the pair admire Amy's first gold record for "Age to Age." When she received the honor it was the first ever awarded to a solo artist in the gospel field.   Photo by John McCormick

bands, Dogwood and Homecoming. There were also a number of top Music City session players like Reggie Young, Shane Keister, Kenny Malone, and Larry London. Amy's voice had none of the nuance and subtlety exhibited on her later records, but she hit most of the notes and the honesty showed through. The songs themselves, half of which were penned by Amy, were the strongest part of the effort. Where most pop LPs feature eight to ten songs, Amy delivered a baker's dozen—thirteen.

The reception given the album by church friends and classmates was universally reinforcing. She became a local hero, yet she could retain her identity as "just Amy": daughter, classmate, Bible study group fellow, and one of the gang at Koinonia. She saw the sales numbers, which would run up to about fifty thousand copies in the first year, but her experience of that success was local, manageable, and fairly undemanding—her friends were happy for her and, aside from isolated invitations to perform for a special group out of town, that's about all she personally experienced of her growing fame.

Just as Amy was beginning to emerge as a touring and recording artist, she also stepped out of high school and into college. Harpeth Hall students had honored Amy with the senior-year superlative "Most Talented" and had recognized her further as Lady of the Hall that year, the quintessential Harpeth Hall girl, but it would soon be time to put those childish days behind her and go on to the more adult atmosphere of college.

Amy's choice of college was Baptist-affiliated Furman University, located at Greenville, South Carolina. Founded as a school to train ministers in 1825, Furman became a full-fledged university in 1859. When Amy strolled onto the campus in September 1978 to begin her studies, she entered a 750-acre world of scenic beauty close by the foot of Paris Mountain, within sight of the Blue Ridge Mountains. A magnificent rose garden, a Japanese garden, and numerous fountains punctuate the campus, which features it's own 30-acre lake and eighteen-hole golf course as prominent landmarks.

Furman, a Christian-oriented university, has a music department in which it takes pride. Amy was undecided on a major study interest until her second year, when she chose English as her major. Tuition, room, and board costs at Furman top $8,000 annually at the undergraduate level, and Amy probably got her money's worth "borrowing" time to work on her songs in the music-department practice rooms. She must have spent many pleasant hours between classes talking with friends in the Palla Den snack bar at Watkins student center, located right next to the lake. There is an Old South grandeur about many of the buildings at Furman, which are faced with handmade Virginia brick and decorated with columned porches.

Away from home, Amy's popularity as a contemporary Christian singer grew, and with it grew the pressures of fame, until they began to impinge on her sense of who she was. After all, she was only seventeen when she had her first hit album. She was young and unprepared for either the process or the attention that followed.

"Oh, I was so embarrassed," she says about the shock of her first serious recording session. "I had never sung for anyone. It came about all backwards."

There had been no years of touring, paying her dues, and honing her craft before the demands and opportunities of incipient stardom began imposing on her life. Amy undoubtedly enjoyed much of the attention she was attracting, but she had to pass through the difficult years of late adolescence under the spotlight of growing fame. She perhaps exaggerated that early spotlight in her own perception, but it was enough to exacerbate things during a period in her life when she seriously questioned who she was and where she was going.

"From the time I was seventeen and a half until my nineteenth birthday I went through an identity crisis because I was claiming something I hadn't laid hold of yet," Amy confessed to gospel authority Don Cusic. "I was splashing around in a big ocean. I didn't accept myself. Something as nebulous and insignificant as a young girl coming up to me at a concert and saying, 'You're not half as pretty as your album covers' or 'Why can't you be more like Evie?' or arriving at a concert and performing hideously with just a piano and guitar and not sounding like my records—it all seeped into my personal life.

"Suddenly I was a basket case. I'd go to a party and wouldn't quite feel comfortable until someone acknowledged I'm a singer because it gave me worth in this life. I would feel a burden to make everyone feel comfortable, because if anyone went away uncomfortable and I was there I felt responsible because I was the public figure. I felt a burden to have everyone like me."

Amy had always been a singularly self-confident person, despite the humorous circumstances of her first recording sessions. Her parents' doting attention in childhood led to her first mini-identity crisis when she entered grammar school and found out that she had to work harder to make strangers laugh than she did her family. Now, far from home and on her own for the first time in her life, the young college freshman was thrown into a more serious identity crisis when she began reading magazine articles about herself in Christian music periodicals. Amy became the subject of numerous glowing reviews and superpositive personality profiles in the fan magazines and youth-ministry publications. Record companies have publicity directors on their payroll whose job is to get stories on artists in the press, painted sometimes in the most unrelentingly hyped colors. She saw her life, music, and personality distilled by strangers into upbeat one-thousand- and two-thousand-word capsules of praiseworthy talent and commitment. The stories read well but they haunted the teen. She knew the hype represented what people wanted to see in her, what they wished her to be.

"What made me so insecure was reading the magazine articles and seeing the image of Amy Grant and then I would look inside and think I'll never measure up to that," Amy explains.

Initial sales of the "Amy Grant" album showed her early appeal and ability to sell records fast. Despite the sincerity of a gospel artist's musical ministry, it is the profit margin that ultimately keeps them on a major label. Gospel music is no different from pop music in that respect. Her record sold about 50,000 copies the first year and eventually passed the 250,000-unit sales mark. Even though the first successes of her recording career were modest by pop or even country standards, they were regarded by the Waco, Texas, executives at Word Records as very promising. The most amazing thing about Amy's sales was that hardly anyone outside the sheltered hollows of Harpeth Hall and Koinonia coffeehouse had ever heard of Amy Grant before.

"Record companies at that time, and even now, want to see the artist tour," explains Wes Yoder, whose pioneering contemporary-Christian-music booking company, Dharma Artist Agency, handled Amy's concerts for nearly two years after she graduated from high school. "Well, this was not a touring artist. It's a classic example of a record company releasing product to see what's going to happen. It's the old throw it up against the wall and it just happened to stick."

The bookstores that belonged to the Christian Booksellers Association (CBA) were a significantly smaller wall to be throwing things at in those days. In business primarily to sell Bibles, Sunday School books, religious greeting cards, and a variety of inspirational and study tomes, CBA stores allocated little space for religious records. Most commercially successful Christian music in earlier years had been gospel collections by stars with secular careers. Acts like

Tennessee Ernie Ford, Johnny Cash, Elvis Presley, and Perry Como, to name a few were affiliated with record labels that had the muscle to place their records in major record shops and department store racks. The expansion of contemporary Christian music as a big-selling item has created demand for CBA record racks.

Word Records may have done little more than send out copies of the record when bookstores ordered it, but Dr. Grant took the business step necessary to assure his daughter's record got a fair chance at success. He hadn't prayed with her backstage before her first Harpeth Hall "show" and many times since just to let Amy's debut record go unheard. As it became apparent to the Grant family that Word wasn't going to spend much effort plugging the album unless it became a smash hit on its own, Amy's father hired an independent promotion man to help whip up interest from Christian bookstores and radio stations which featured special contemporary Christian music programs in response to a growing trend toward gospel music.

Amy's remarkable early success brought an invitation from the Gospel Music Association for her to appear on stage during the Gospel Music Association Dove Awards ceremonies. Held in Nashville, the Dove Awards Show is the high point of the biggest single annual gathering of the gospel music trade. Glad as she was to be included in her newly found musical family, she soon found that among most other gospel professionals, even those her own age, she stood out like the parson's new stepdaughter.

"I remember the first time I went to a GMA Awards event," Amy says. "I was seventeen and I was presenting an award. I didn't know anybody. I didn't know any of their names. I had one album out. I was presenting an award with three other girls. We sat down and they were really nice, but they were all talking about people they knew. They just knew everybody. It seemed like everybody knew everybody.

"Some of it was by virtue that some of them were from

family groups and had played so many festivals together. But it was at that point I realized this is a world unto itself. It really is. And you know, 'What family do you sing with?' was the first question I was asked. They dated each other's brothers and sisters and I was so intrigued. Here I was, I'd just graduated from this girls' prep school. This was so foreign. It seemed as though people were satisfied for it to be an alternative musical universe."

Amy was never satisfied to simply accept the limits of that self-truncated universe. The songs on "Amy Grant" have more in common with pop songs and folk tunes of the late seventies than with the hymns, emotive praise songs, and Bible-oriented music of most of the late-seventies gospel music industry establishment. Gloria Grant reports that Amy's fantasy during her early teen years was to sing professionally the songs she was singing at home and at school. By the time she made her first GMA Awards Show appearance, her growing repertoire was already stylistically miles away from those of gospel quartets and family acts.

To be sure, the contemporary Christian movement was by that time strongly represented within the gospel music industry, but Amy would never be completely comfortable limiting herself to strictly evangelistic subject matter. If anything, she was still bewildered that she had wound up a gospel singer in the first place.

About the time Amy packed her steamer trunk for Furman, a family conference that included brother-in-law Dan Harrell gave Amy guidance on continuing with her singing, but kept her mind mainly on her studies. Since her first year of college meshed with her first year as a budding gospel music star, on the road two weekends a month, Amy tried to integrate these elements of her young life by taking a college chum along for company on many of her concert trips. Amy identifies her first serious concert as taking place in July 1978 after her high school graduation. That performance took place at the Lakeside Amusement Park in Denver, Colorado. She subsequently traveled to college-sponsored coffeehouses and youth forums in the Southeast and Rocky Mountain states. Her mother was an early "road manager," really more a chaperone occasionally going with her youngest daughter. Amy was surprising even herself with the effect she and her guitar had on an audience of young people. This early reception served to cement the Grant family's support of her budding career.

"After her first album the people from Word called us and asked us to go on a two-week tour," recalls Gloria Grant. "I went with Amy and when I came back I told my husband, 'Burton, this child has a purpose in life.' I felt that because she was put in positions she wasn't prepared for and I saw how beautifully she responded. She never seemed frazzled or at a loss for the right comment. You know, when she's talking to you there could be a hundred other people there, but if she's talking to you, you don't feel like there's anybody there but you and Amy. She has a gift for making each person feel important."

Still, in her first year Amy had little confidence or power on stage. In the beginning, Amy's performance was certainly less than kinetic. It was just Amy sitting on a stool at center stage, strumming her guitar and singing the songs that had come from her heart. Chatting about the feelings behind her songs, sharing a few stories about herself, she was learning to establish a rough, but genuine rapport. She sometimes filled out her sound by carrying tapes of her studio tracks and performed her songs accompanied by a tape recorder that recreated the music of her album with the eerie exactness of a phantom band. In those early days of coffeehouse and college concerts her Christian repertoire was pretty slim.

"When I first started doing concerts I didn't have to go on the road because there wasn't any big demand for me," Amy recalls. "People would just call about once a month and ask if I could come to their place and sing. I'd pack up my guitar and just fly out there. It has really only been [since 1980 or 1981] that I've done any real touring at all. But one of the first concerts I can remember doing I had one thousand kids show up at the Will Rogers Memorial Auditorium in Fort Worth, Texas.

"I had no idea how the promoter did that. I knew maybe three people in Fort Worth and couldn't understand how the promoter got one thousand people there. I hardly knew any songs. I just knew the songs I'd written plus maybe five or six more. I remember playing everything I knew and I'd only played for like fifty-five minutes and I finally said, 'I don't know any more songs.' But the kids yelled from the balcony, 'Why don't you just sing your songs over again?' It was so informal. I just said okay and started singing 'em over again."

For an unknown, Amy had done well by filling more than one third of the 2,964 seats of the Fort Worth auditorium. Amy's career, for that's what it was becoming by the time she got to the Furman University campus in the autumn of 1978, had been directed in large part by family consensus. Far from pushing her into singing, they tended to shelter her at every turn, spending family resources where necessary to underwrite the efforts she wanted to make. The importance of family agreement remained paramount during her most formative years, but brother-in-law Dan Harrell had begun taking a larger role in the decision-making part of her career. The "Amy Grant" sales results suggested to him that if her music could find such a big audience by little more than word-of-mouth promotion, she had potential requiring greater professional attention and direction. She was obviously too young, inexperienced in business, and even ambivalent about becoming a star to make the difficult decisions on her own.

Chris Christian and, increasingly, Brown Bannister had control over how her records would sound. They had their own ideas about how Christian music could have the same aural impact as a good rock or pop record. Driving beats and sizzling electric guitars marked their esthetic. Amy's tastes were eclectic, but her experience was limited. Bannister sometimes had to give her a nudge in the direction he thought her music should go. Amy's experience with her third album, "Never Alone," solidified his role.

"We did a song called 'Too Late' and I was out of town when they did the guitar solo," Amy explains. "I came back and I thought, ugh, it sounds like drug music. It was so dark-sounding . . . I'm still not wild about that solo."

Her idea of drug music was just a common rock 'n' roll sound effect added to the guitar solo. Though someone else had the reins with her music, she has always had important input on the tunes picked for her records.

"There are a group of us that chooses," she says, "but I've never been asked to do or sing anything that I wasn't a supporter of."

Her father had been important in the management of her high school-days career, such as it was. Dan Harrell, a young banker married to Amy's older sister Kathy, stepped in to control the details of her developing career after the success of "Amy Grant." Harrell had six years of banking experience behind him at Tennessee's largest bank, First Tennessee, and he had previously worked in television as a production coordinator for Screen Gems's early-seventies weekly variety program starring Johnny Cash. More than anyone else in the extended family, Harrell had an idea of the media aspect of what the future could hold for Amy.

"He was my banker and he always asked me questions about how the music business worked," says Rick Bolsom, editor of *Country Song Roundup* magazine and a former rock music manager. "He was a nice guy, he asked real direct questions, and he learned real quick."

Harrell stands just under six feet, a burly man in his mid-thirties with short, cropped black hair and a ready smile. His experience and proximity to both the gospel and country entertainment communities in Nashville gave him a hunch that he might carve a niche for himself on the business end of the burgeoning contemporary Christian music field.

Harrell and the Grant family initially approved Amy's concert arrangements through a booking agent named Dan Brock. They soon switched to the Dharma Artist Agency, with the idea that Amy's education was a priority and she would only perform two weekends per month. They also decided that she would stay away from fundamentalist-church-sponsored concerts, because her music was no more likely to find acceptance there than had any previous contemporary Christian act.

"We've always worked with the colleges because contemporary Christian music wasn't at first embraced widely by the church," explains Yoder. "So we didn't start out working with a wide network of churches that embraced us, we were rock and roll from the beginning."

Much as her career can be made to appear the perfect Cinderella story, there were some hard times on those early tours. Amy wasn't always the darling of all promoters, especially during her freshman year in college.

"It didn't go well at all," she recalls. "I wasn't getting through to my audiences. One booker saw me on stage and canceled. I was getting more nervous each time I performed."

With so few chances to polish her approach to an audience, Amy simply prayed, tried to gulp down her nervousness, and opened herself up to her audiences. Sometimes she didn't come off too well, finding out for the second time in her young life that strangers aren't entertained as easily or by the same things that draw applause from one's family. Strangers who paid hard cash for seats at her concerts were a different kind of audience than her Harpeth Hall classmates dressed in plaid skirted uniforms and pulling for their Lady of the Hall.

Perhaps Amy tried to "give a show" in that original tour. For Amy Grant, that would have been faking it. More likely, it was the lack of consistent and frequent chances to perform that slowed her development of stage savvy. Religion was the key to gaining confidence enough to open herself up to audiences, to again become the vulnerable, open, and honest young lady who had made them all cry at the high school devotional.

"I had a dream," she says. "I dreamed I was in heaven and God put His arm around me and said, 'Amy, what have you done for me?' I had my album behind my back and said, 'Look, Lord, I've been singing for you. Here's my album.' He was a little disappointed. That's when I woke up and realized I was a little too proud of myself and that my whole life at that time was just a piece of plastic, a round record."

Amy gained confidence by forgetting her own self-consciousness for a while, but she was still concerned that she was technically not as good a singer as some of the other people she met around Nashville. Being a major recording center, Nashville draws the very best vocalists and musicians. She credits backup singer Donna McElroy, who sings in Amy's vocal group on the road, with teaching her how to increase her projection and control. Another Nashville-based contemporary Christian entertainer, Steve Camp, reportedly gets some of the credit for helping her be more expressive with her stage movements, encouraging her to dance around to the beat. Even when her voice had the tentative qualities of her inexperience she still had the magic of projecting her sincerity. Her rapport with an audience has been a strength, once she learned from experience to trust it.

"One of the things about Amy that makes her so attractive is her incredible transparency, just laying her life down before people," says Don Finto. "It sometimes gets her in trouble in the way she words herself or the way people quote her as wording herself. They put words in her mouth.

It sometimes works against her but it's also her strength. She gets before a concert and she just tells things about herself that most people wouldn't tell. She just unveils herself before people to let them know she is a person just like they are. That's part of her strength."

That strength was intuitive, so completely natural that she didn't fully comprehend the power she could wield over an audience with her openness and frankness. She projected the traits of innocence and openness, but it still puzzled her that audiences would laugh or cry just because she shared stories about her childhood, her concerns and joys of the present in a context of her Christian faith. Her show wasn't what she thought of when she imagined professional showmen like her old heroes Elton John, Carole King, and James Taylor. A developing professional, Amy worried about how she sounded.

"I was very scared [at first] because I don't have a Barbra Streisand voice," she explains. "I'm not the kind of person that can get up and sing one song and blow an audience away. When in the position to sing three songs, my fear comes from the fact that I don't have that kind of voice. I went with a large church group one time. I went to be a special guest and I had three songs right in the middle of their performance. They started talking about the last person that had done a three-song set and he'd sung three songs and gotten three standing ovations.

"So, okay, I'm eighteen, on a Learjet flying to Mobile. I'm thinking, he got three standing ovations in three songs. I don't think I've ever gotten a standing ovation from one song. I don't like for it to be a moment-to-moment reaction to an artist. I never even expect that anybody will stand up after a song so I don't have that pressure. I'd rather have it that way."

Amy turned eighteen in the middle of her first semester at Furman. During that freshman year at college, Amy struggled through personal anxieties and found being a student and a traveling musician a tiring combination. In the hearts of contemporary Christian music fans she was rapidly filling the vacuum being left by Evie Tornquist. Evie still records, but her pixie-cut blonde hair and dimpled smile were being seen less frequently on the road as she turned toward the ministry and her husband's Swedish homeland.

Because Furman was a Christian-oriented university, Amy's growing fame was probably better known among students there than it would have been at most secular institutions of higher learning. She notes the support she got from her freshman hall, G-200, in the liner notes of her second album, "My Father's Eyes." Still, contemporary Christian music was largely a creature of the ghetto of parachurch youth organizations such as Young Life. A gospel singer could be a completely unknown commodity to the mainstream American music fan. It all kept her a little on edge.

"I have a wonderful sense of insecurity about myself," says Amy. "It's what keeps me on my toes."

She conquered her studies and struggled through her touring schedule, learning how to handle herself with crowds slowly, but surely. She dated lightly, seeing different young men in either South Carolina or Nashville. But the need to be in Nashville many weekends for recording sessions meant there was little time for deep attachments that 1978–79 school year.

Sales of the "Amy Grant" album continued to mount, stoked by Dr. Grant's independent record promoter and widely spreading word-of-mouth recommendations. Satisfied that they had an artist with potential on their hands, Word Records approved a budget for a second album. Word Inc.'s wider interests in music publishing recognized the appeal of Amy's music to amateur musicians, so an *Amy Grant Songbook* was also issued.

During the 1978–79 school year, her first year of serious

concerts, she was on the verge of her big breakthrough. Brown Bannister took her back into the studio to record her second album. There were some new touches to the Gold Mine sound room, and there were a growing number of young songwriters interested in having their tunes cut by the rising star. One of the most important for Amy was the young son of a Texas minister, the writer of her second album's title song, Gary Chapman.

Chapter 7

Twenty-year-old Gary Chapman was hungry for his first taste of success and songwriting royalties when the word went out among the gospel song publishing community that Brown Bannister and Word's artist and repertoire man Mike Blanton were listening to tunes for Amy Grant's second album. Born August 19, 1957, in Waurika, Oklahoma, Chapman was seven when the Reverend T. W. Chapman moved the family to De Leon, Texas. Gary was raised around all-day sings and dinners on the grounds that Texas congregations made after-church affairs on many summer Sundays. He picked up his first guitar almost as soon as he got to Texas and taught himself to play by slowing Chet Atkins records down to half-speed until he could follow the master picker note for note.

He gathered musical influences from those gospel-singing marathons and from country and pop stations whose signals wafted across the Texas prairie. It seemed to Gary as he grew into his teens that there wasn't much he couldn't do musically, if he only put his mind to it. When he was nineteen, he got his first professional experience as a guitarist for a popular traditional gospel group called the Downings. He soon realized how much hard work and sacrifice had to go into achieving his aspirations.

Chapman had attended the Southwestern Assemblies of God College in Waxahachie, Texas, but he was hardly a scholar.

"I don't think I ever really went to college," Chapman confesses. "I was just there. I hung around the dorm a lot and made a lot of friends, but I didn't really go to school."

When Chapman joined the Downings, he moved to Nashville with the act. Four months later the job ended. He had not saved much money so he returned to school, mostly for a haven, since he still had no intention of becoming a pulpit preacher. Nominally in school in Texas, Chapman realized he wanted a career in music more than anything else. When friendships he made in the gospel music industry later led to an offer from one of gospel music's bigger family acts, the Rambos, he moved back to Nashville, determined to stick it out this time. He was working, but he sure wasn't getting rich or famous overnight.

"I lived on crackers for at least a year," Chapman claims, tongue-in-cheek. "I was into singing and playing at the time and I did not begin to mature as a writer until I started playing guitar on the road with the Rambos. Listening to Dottie Rambo's writing—I just started to view songs differently—as a craft.

"I was really captured by the way Dottie constructed her songs. I never knew there was that much to it. It's like the words are all there and you have to get them in the right order."

Nashville has come a long way from those days in the 1940s when Roy Acuff and Fred Rose opened Nashville's first country music publishing company. A lone songwriter, pounding the pavement of Music Row with country or gospel tunes to peddle, is at a disadvantage compared to a tunesmith affiliated with a publisher. The lone tunesmith has fewer tunes to offer than does a vast catalog of a major publisher, which may represent hundreds of talented writers. Publishers, by virtue of constantly presenting songs, develop personal contacts with artists, record company executives, and record producers that individual writers cannot make. Publishers also have money for expensive demonstration sessions for songs they believe in.

In earlier years, Nashville was the last great bastion of the free-lance songwriter who needed only talent, a guitar, and a notepad to write lyrics. The complexities of the growing music industry in the past ten years changed all that. As country and gospel music began to surge in popularity in the late seventies, an absolute flood of hopeful songwriters poured over Music Row. The number of bad songs available increased geometrically each time a Greyhound bus pulled in carrying yet another load of guitar-playing drifters hawking hackneyed tunes and rhymes lifted from dimestore greeting cards.

Artists and producers no longer had time to listen to the multiplying volume of unsolicited songs that came across their transoms, nor did they wish to risk the pesky copyright infringement lawsuits that became more common in the 1970s. Defending such a nuisance suit, as cases that are unfounded are called, could cost more than the royalties from a Top Twenty country tune, much less most gospel songs.

Having a policy of accepting unsolicited material became a legal liability. With so many new Christian songwriters arriving in Nashville every day, there just wasn't time for acts and their producers to listen to every stranger who asked for their ear. Artists and producers became increasingly reticent to let people they didn't personally know pitch them songs. The growing gospel music business was taking some cues in this respect from their next door neighbors, the country music industry. Gary pestered Paragon Music Corporation song plugger Randy Cox until he finally got an appointment to present his tunes. When the offer to join the roster at Paragon came, Gary balked at first.

"I was skeptical," Chapman recalls, "I had all those

small-town fears of being ripped off and it took me a month to decide to sign."

Cox not only signed Chapman, he championed the young singer/songwriter to various Christian record companies. Mike Blanton, head of A&R (Artists and Repertoire) at the Word Inc. Nashville office, wanted to sign Chapman to the Word Records family, perhaps to Myrhh/Word, the same sublabel that Amy Grant was on. Before any such deal could be arranged, Blanton was invited to join Dan Harrell in business. Blanton and Harrell had become friends through the Belmont Church and because of their joint faith in Amy Grant's potential. Cox continued to look for a record label to sign Chapman to, and, to Chapman's amazement, Paragon actually gave him extra money to renew his writer's contract with them after the first one-year deal ran out.

A few years later, Chapman and Cox jointly left Paragon to become seed talent for Meadowgreen Music, the newly established gospel wing of Tree International, one of Nashville's biggest and oldest pop and country music publishers. Tree has the biggest roster of songwriters in Nashville. It sometimes numbers as many as sixty writers whose talents usually lean toward the pop music side of Nashville's country recording scene. All these writers were jockeying to get time in the multitrack, demo-recording studio that Tree owner Buddy Killen had built at the heart of his four-story office complex on Music Row. Tree writers have to schedule demo sessions weeks in advance, but part of Chapman's perks for signing with Meadowgreen was a shot at the twenty-four-track studio within his first week there.

One tune that Chapman quickly demoed at the Tree studio was called "Finally." Its melody was an excellent , pop/country tune and the words suitably ambivalent so that it could be taken as a man-woman love song or a song of born-again religious experience. Country music singer T. G. Sheppard (stage name for Bill Browder, which coincidentally stands for The Good Shepherd) took the position that people would interpret the lyrics according to their own bias. This was a key insight into the resulting success of the whole pop-gospel trend toward light religious references and strong pop melodies. Sheppard, a very popular artist at his peak, recorded "Finally" and it became one of his biggest hits, going all the way to *Billboard* magazine's Number One spot in 1982.

There were undoubtedly pressures on Gary to devote more time to writing tunes for the commercially rewarding country/pop market. He certainly had no compunction against doing so, but he preferred to pursue his own contemporary Christian recordings. Seeing his opportunity to become a recording artist in the contemporary Christian ranks, Chapman resisted the pressures to produce more country/pop hits as his own recording career seemed to be taking off. Gary signed with Lamb & Lion Records, a label owned by Pat Boone, which had an active office in Nashville.

Randy Cox originally signed Gary Chapman to Paragon on the strength of a song called "Father's Eyes." The beautiful, mid-tempo tune features lyrics that evoke nostalgia for one's parent as well as sentimental desire to reflect God's love in some way, if only in the way one views the world. The contemporary Christian music industry was on the verge of tremendous nationwide growth. Cox could almost feel that excitement in the air as he walked through Music Row to Mike Blanton's office with a tape of Chapman's song in his hand. If Amy Grant was the girl vocalist in the right place at the right time to catch that wave of expansion in the Christian music world, Cox had to believe that Chapman had just brought him the song to make it happen for her. It was "the right stuff" she absolutely had to have if being in the right place at the right time was going to pay off. If Amy broke out to the head of the crowd with his song, everyone involved would benefit.

When Mike Blanton and Brown Bannister played "Father's Eyes" for Amy the first time, she cried. The song moved her deeply, firing her producer's conviction that it would do the same for the teens and young adults who bought most contemporary Christian records. The song formed the basis for the title song of Amy's second album, "My Father's Eyes."

"Little did I know when I recorded ["Father's Eyes"] that I would one day be the wife of the man who wrote it," Amy quips.

Brown Bannister's improved production values set a higher standard for the second album. Pop horn sounds like those the group Chicago uses, rhythmic intimations of the Bee Gees, and lush string arrangements mark some of these songs. There is a variety of musical styles and feelings on the record, including, among Amy's contributions, one of her own compositions, "Always the Winner." This song is a wistful, string-laden lament about the ego temptations that show business was already starting to inflict on her. A somewhat autobiographical song, its lyrics tell of a girl at the center of attention who gets lonely when the crowds go home. Amy recognized that growing fame had the potential to put her, rather than the message she wanted to get across, into the forefront.

There are special moments on this album, including guest appearances by Amy's three older sisters, who have lovely voices, though they are not professional singers. Kathy Harrell, Mimi Verner, and Carol Grant (now Nuismer) participated as backup singers on an ancient classical hymn called "O Sacred Head," composed by Hans Hassler and harmonized by J. S. Bach. The recording session for "O Sacred Head" came dangerously close to exceeding Amy's scheduled time in Nashville one weekend; it was 4 A.M. on a late winter's night when she finished singing and she was due to drive back to Furman the next day.

The beautiful a cappella harmonies must have carried the

Grant sisters back to their Church of Christ childhood, when singing God's music always meant voices without instrumental accompaniment. Listeners the age of Amy's oldest sister, in her late thirties, or parents could find the Grant girls' combined sound reminiscent of the Lennon Sisters, four winsome Midwest girls whose wholesome harmonies made them stars (from 1955 to 1968) on Lawrence Welk's weekly television show.

Four men's voices add bottom to the vocal mix on the hymn starting about halfway through, but it was a late-night/early-morning brainstorm by Brown Bannister, combined with a thunderstorm outside the studio, that really provided an eerie complement to the track. Thunderclaps, low, deep, and rumbling in from the distance, were captured on the tape the first time Bannister stuck his microphone into the rainy night. He had expected to record the quiet splatter of raindrops on the driveway for a soothing background sound, but thunder serendipitously clapped three times: to herald the girls' first notes, to accent a line that describes Jesus's crucifixion when He is subject to abuse and scorn, and at the exact moment the song ends. Brown attributes the magnificently timed "nature track" to Divine orchestration.

Amy wrote or cowrote eight of the thirteen tunes that appear on "My Father's Eyes." Her songwriting credits were expanded for more collaboration with Brown Bannister. The songs by both Amy and Bannister were published by Chris Christian's Bug and Bear Music Company. Any royalties collected by the American Society of Composers and Publishers (ASCAP) for radio air play or mechanical royalties for copies sold would typically have been split on a 50/50 basis, with the publisher earning half and each writer collecting an equal part of the 50 percent writers' share. That deal is the music industry norm. There are regulated payments from performance royalties for air play, negotiated between the broadcasters and such performing rights organizations as ASCAP, Broadcast Music Incorporated (BMI), and SESAC. Record companies are bound by the statutory royalty rate set by the 1976 Copyright Tribunal to pay the people who own songs 4½ cents per song, per copy sold. Songwriters and publishers divide up these pennies, which can quickly add up when a record becomes a big seller.

Luckily, Amy didn't have to live off her meager early earnings. Her family situation gave her an advantage no other contemporary gospel act enjoyed. While her early earnings went to support management, promotion, and publicity activities, Dr. Grant footed her living expenses, since she was still a dependent college student.

Her parents never stinted on either moral support or financial generosity for Amy's career. Not the least of their early support was the services of that professional record plugger to promote "Amy Grant." In keeping with the Grant family's mutual generosity, she was returning the favor.

"Let me tell you what Amy did when she first started writing songs and getting a few royalties," Amy's mother says. "One year at Christmas she gave each one of her sisters one of her songs. They each get a royalty off it twice a year."

The sisters' names do not appear as writers on any of the album jacket credits and no one in the family or management team has revealed which songs they are. Given the continued, steady sales of her albums, Amy's gift of songwriter credits has undoubtedly been worth hundreds of dollars to her sisters and will continue to ring up royalties, as long as her records stay in print. Amy's generosity to her sisters is a quiet, personal thing among the tightly knit family.

Considering the non-impression he made on Amy when they met for the first time in the spring of 1979, it's a wonder that Gary Chapman ever got to be a member of the family. Since he had written her biggest hit tune up to that time, one might expect their introduction to have registered as something special. From his perspective, at least, it did.

"[It was] one of the first things I ever tried to sell as a songwriter," says Gary. "Amy cut the song and we met at an album-listening party."

She thanked him for writing the song and letting her have it to record. There was chit-chat, a cup of punch or soft drink to toast good luck, and God's blessing on the record, and that was that. Amy did not know it yet, but according to Gary, it was love at first sight.

"I decided the day I met her," Chapman remembers. "She knocked me out that day."

He knew in 1979 she was only eighteen, while he was twenty-one, but her fresh-faced preppy beauty simply dazzled him.

"I called her that night and from that point on I tastefully pursued her," he says with a grin.

Actually, Amy was somewhat offended by Gary's initial attentions. She had another beau and recalls Gary's first approach violated her sense of loyalty to her boyfriend.

"He asked me for a date," Amy says. "I liked somebody at the time and said no. I flew back to South Carolina, where I was a freshman in college. He called me on the phone and apologized. He said he knew I was dating but he thought he'd give it a stab. I thought he was an interesting fellow to call back."

The first completely secular love song from Amy's own pen, "I Love You" from the album "Unguarded," delves into the wild impetuousness with which Chapman pursued Amy after that. That pursuit seems to have been rather one-sided because Amy recalls that they didn't see each other again for about six months. She was traveling to concerts two weeks a month and often flew back to Nashville to record and visit her family on other weekends.

"He'd send tapes and notes, 'Here's your next hit song,'" Amy explains. "I thought he was joking and I'd write back the song was weak. He lost all respect for my musical opinions."

If Amy was somewhat naive about Gary Chapman's attentions and attempts to impress her with his talent and humor, it was in large part because communication at a distance kept his wild personal charm from reaching her directly. He is flip, and quick-witted, while his music shows a more serious side that is not otherwise widely revealed. Letters and phone calls just don't have the same effect as close personal proximity, where a sweet compliment can be amplified with emotion by even the most innocent touch on the arm or lingering eye contact. Amy had little spare time in which to contemplate the long-distance attentions of the songwriter. She was too busy trying to fit her studies and campus life into five-day weeks so she could dash around the country on tour or back to Nashville to take care of career business.

The broadening experience of travel and work in the exciting atmosphere of talented writers, musicians, and producers put a lot of distance between Amy and her Furman classmates. She had friends there, but few whose lives matched her own experiences. This gulf between her own vista-broadening life-style and those of campus-bound college freshmen made her somewhat lonely at school, even in a crowd. At home, she found she could tell about her Furman life but not fully share it with anyone in Nashville. It depressed her and sent her into deep moments of wondering who she really was.

"I was still going to school, majoring in English at Furman University in South Carolina," Amy recalls. "That was kind of a rough time for me."

Popping in and out of the radically different worlds of college and the concert trail as she did hardly helped the young girl's identity quandaries. The pressures of flying back to Nashville every spare weekend to record her second album added to her oppressively busy work load, but being in the studio also offered the stimulation of creating new music. There, too, some of the pressure was removed. On stage or during an important college exam, Amy was on her own to succeed or fail, but in the cavelike confines of Gold Mine studio Amy and Brown Bannister enjoyed the option of endless retakes and the confidence of eventual perfection.

"Back then I had this idea that I had to deliver one album every year at the same time," she recounts. "It was sort of like having four babies in four years. With going to school and all, I was exhausted."

Most of the business pressures on Amy, particularly those regarding concert dates, were deflected by Dan Harrell, who had quit his job with First Tennessee Bank by then and become Amy's full-time manager. He reportedly received some financial aid in the beginning from Dr. Grant. Amy's father is a businessman, as well as a physician. His eye for winning propositions in Nashville had already included investments in the local Bonanza Steak House franchise and *Nashville Magazine*. Dr. Grant's investment criterion, at least as far as these particular investments were concerned, seemed to have the common thread of backing relatives. Daughter Mimi Grant Verner's husband Jerry was involved in top-level management of the steak-house franchise, while nephew Wilson Burton was a founder of *Nashville Magazine*.

Harrell directed Dharma Artist Agency, which would handle her booking arrangements through the spring of 1980, to screen requests for Amy's live performances in order to keep her from getting overexposed as a young artist. She also needed as much time as possible for school and recording. Dharma's Wes Yoder remembers that by her sophomore year, Amy was asked to play much more often than Harrell's development schedule allowed.

"Most of what our job consisted of then was turning down dates," Dharma Agency's head man recalls.

Harrell's plan was to create a demand for Amy's concerts, but not to fully satisfy that demand until it built up to bigger profit potential. If they wanted her now, they would want her even more the next year. Harrell also decided early on that Amy, as a contemporary Christian singer with few hymns in her repertoire, should avoid the established route for gospel singers. Her concert dates primarily skipped churches, revivals, and the like, which are the mainstay of the traditional gospel road to visibility. He was able to stick to his wise plan in part because of Dr. Grant's early financial support. Because Amy didn't need the money derived from the concerts, it could all go to keeping the management and publicity company going. Nobody else in the history of gospel music has come from such a comfortable background that the short-range need for making a living didn't color long-range planning early in the game. The financial cushion allowed them to treat Amy very much in the manner of the pop music industry. They were able to choose concert locations and dates to their own best advantage in making an end run around the traditional gospel channels. The fact that neither Dan Harrell nor Mike Blanton had business backgrounds in the traditional gospel music industry contributed to the tack they took with Amy's career.

"They were young and business-wise," explains GMA's Don Butler. "Mike Blanton was in charge of Word Record's Nashville office, he took care of recording details for them here. Dan Harrell was a banker. They designed a formula and stuck with it, with their goals for Amy clearly in sight. They are more responsible for her success than anything else. Of course they were Christians, high-principled, but not so dogmatic as not to see the possibilities of reaching out with music as the message. They have done things differently than the normal gospel agencies and management teams, from the way they promoted Amy to controlling the venues and types of interviews and media exposure she got."

The success of "Father's Eyes," which grew through 1979 to become the most popular gospel tune of the year, according to the Gospel Music Association's twelfth annual Dove Awards vote tally, spurred demand for Amy's concerts. Even more promoters and student activities committees wanted to book her to sing. Demand reached a major breakthrough point in the spring semester of her sophomore year at Furman.

"I remember the first really big thing that happened was a weekend we put together in the Pacific Northwest," recalls Yoder. "She played Portland, Seattle, and Spokane. I think all three of them were sellouts with about two thousand or twenty-five hundred people at each place. We had a great promoter and everything working right. It was the shot where we could tell it was going to take off from there."

The previously one-sided romance between Gary and Amy was about to take off, as well. Despite all his phone calls and the tapes he mailed to her at Furman, Gary had not made a very vivid impression on the eighteen-year-old pop-gospel thrush. They had run into each other earlier, hanging out at the Koinonia bookstore/coffeehouse, visiting with friends, and taking turns on the short stage at the end of the long, narrow room. Despite Gary's attempts to win Amy's attention during the year after they were first formally introduced, she hardly remembered him. He may have been "cruising" her in his own mind, but sparks were only flying in one direction.

While Amy appears to have been oblivious to Chapman's long-term romantic intentions, he nonetheless knew what his own feelings were. She was different. Her world of private schools and protected suburbs was far removed from the modest little Texas hometown of his parents, the

Reverend T. W. and Mary Chapman. Amy had an un-
spoiled beauty, an awkward, gawky gracefulness animated
by a seemingly unending source of nervous energy. Even a
plain-faced person is rendered attractive by an aura of self-
confidence and the kind of nonjudgmental openness that
invites others to reach down and present their own best
side—and Amy was by no means plain.

The facial features that make Amy Grant a standout come
predominantly from her father. His own deep eyes and
shiny round cheeks make him look a little like a youthful
Santa Claus. Her slight body may more closely resemble
Gloria Grant's trim physique, but Amy most definitely has
her father's eyes. Those twinkling brown orbs are deep and
sincere, providing the looks to match that honest vulnera-
bility. Her long, frizzy, permed brown hair and widow's
peaked forehead give her away in a crowd, but face-to-face
or from the back of an auditorium, it is her eyes that compel
one's attention. They certainly captured Gary Chapman,
who was close enough to realize that the physical manifes-
tations of wide-eyed innocence that attracted concertgoers
were an accurate reflection of her true, unaffected nature.
He could resist her instantly likable earnestness even less
than the fans.

"She was so naive," Chapman recalls of his early impres-
sions of his wife. "Not spacey exactly, but vulnerable."

Amy, the beautiful, religiously intense but otherwise
lighthearted, wide-eyed innocent, wasn't tuned in for serious romance in her late teen's and early twenties. Because
she looked so deeply into things she was immediately concerned about—religion and music at that moment—she
ignored the subtle inroads Chapman was trying to make. By
the time Dan Harrell suggested that Gary Chapman become her opening act for the 1980 summer concert tour,
she had almost completely misplaced him in her mind.

"Gary used to drop by occasionally to play a few songs,"
Amy recalls. "He seemed nice enough, but the next year

when my manager said he wanted to put me on the road with Gary Chapman, I couldn't place his name."

The strength of his own growing career as a songwriter and his energetic performing style—rather than his flirtations with Amy—crossed his path with hers that fateful summer. This time they would get to know each other well and their friendship would grow into a deeper, shared affection.

"The summer after my sophomore year, my brother-in-law and his partner, who managed me, decided Gary should do a warmup act for my concerts," Amy says. "They'd seen him perform somewhere."

Mike Blanton was well aware of Chapman's talents as a singer and songwriter. Blanton had wanted to sign him in a publishing and recording deal while he was still at Word Records. Chapman wound up with Lamb & Lion Records because he preferred to maintain his publishing relationship with Randy Cox. Cox was still at Paragon Music when it was absorbed by gospel music giant the Benson Company, which had a pressing and distribution deal with the Pat Boone-owned record label. The new "family" relationship linking the Paragon publishing catalog and Lamb & Lion Records made it easier for Chapman to get a recording deal.

"Lamb & Lion's office was about four doors down the hall from mine at Benson once we moved over there," Cox recalls. "I didn't have far to go to present Gary to them."

When Mike Blanton became Dan Harrell's partner, he continued his interest in Gary Chapman. Regardless of Blanton's inability to put together a publishing and recording deal for the young writer/singer, Blanton and Harrell recognized his talent and potential. They moved to manage his career at about the same time he entered a Memphis studio to cut his first album for Lamb & Lion. It naturally followed that they would want him to be exposed to the same big crowds who were flocking to see their premier act, Amy Grant.

Blanton and Harrell also knew Chapman as a fellow member of Belmont Church, where Chapman was one of a growing number of talented young contemporary Christian writers contributing their music to the eclectic worship service conducted each Sunday morning and evening. They knew a great deal about Chapman, but they didn't know he was secretly smitten by Amy.

Once the addition of Chapman to the tour schedule was confirmed, Amy decided to invite him for a few days' visit to Furman at the end of that spring.

"I was back in school then, so I invited him up for the weekend to get to know him," she recalls. "It wasn't romantic at all. We played racquetball, sang together, and went for drives in the country. We started finding things we both enjoyed doing together."

As they began her accelerated summer concert schedule together, they would find even more.

Chapter 8

Amy and Gary spent long hours together both on and off the road that summer. Chapman's warmth and wit were winning one heart in the wings along with all the hearts and souls he was winning over in the audience. Amy learned a lot about performing by watching Chapman's timing and humor. And Gary couldn't help but notice the forthright honesty which magnified Amy's charismatic rapport with her audience. In front of the largest crowd, a thirty-thousand-strong festival of young people held in Kissimmee, Florida, Amy blurted out something to the crowd of high school and college students that immediately tore down all the barriers of pretense which an elevated stage and musical message can create. She told them that she was horny.

"We're sitting there, I do my sound check. All these girls are in halter tops, great figures, everybody's wearing nothing, we're in Florida," Amy says. "I'm eighteen and I know what they're thinking. I said, 'I really want to know Jesus and I really want to love him except . . . my hormones are on ten and I see you all . . . sitting out there getting chummy and praying together—and we're horny. My feeling is why fake it? I'm not trying to be gross, I'm saying let's be honest about what's coming down. Do you want to get to know Jesus? Fine. Let's be honest about who we are.'"

By the time that episode surfaced in print in the summer of 1985, nobody in the gospel industry thought any more of her comments than to say, "There she goes again." Her penchant for flabbergasting friends and foes alike with juicy quotes that appear in the press, oblivious to the more staid image preferred by the more tradition-bound in the gospel world, is an established part of her legend. In the summer of 1981, though, such unintentionally incongruous statements were adding a new ingredient to the contemporary Christian concert circuit.

Gary and Amy were getting to know each other and enjoying many shared experiences. Driving into the nearby countryside was one of their favorite pastimes. On a few of their many automobile forays through the rolling green hills of middle Tennessee, Gary shared with Amy the gothic wonders of Mount Olivet, one of Nashville's oldest and most imposing cemeteries. He, like the great poet Edgar Lee Masters, found inspiration for his writing among the time-worn, moss-etched granite tombstones and monuments.

"It's quiet, that's one thing," he explains. "But there's more to it than that. Getting close to death gives me a clearer perspective on life. It triggers my imagination."

Amy and Gary quickly developed a fiery, intense relationship characterized at times by smooth sailing, happy and sharing days when the synergy of their talents and individual joys of life made the concert trail tremendously fulfilling. On other days their relationship was marked by disagreements arising from the differences in perspective they each brought from disparate backgrounds. Despite the disagreements, the attraction between them grew.

"It was a lot of fun," Amy says. "You can't put a nineteen-year-old and a twenty-two-year-old together for that long a time without there being some kind of interaction. We could have been any two kids out doing what we both loved to do. The results would have been the same."

Still, Amy did not define their growing relationship as L-O-V-E. Although she used that word in her reminiscence of those days of their first joint tour, it was a more tentative feeling.

"In a working situation we saw the best and the worst of each other," she recalls. "We really liked each other and kind of fell in love."

She had no idea just how taken Gary Chapman was with her.

"I guess I didn't realize he was courting," she confesses. "I thought we were great friends, that's all. He became a part of my family. They took him in because they thought he was just a companion to their little girl. It was pretty sneaky."

There were professional as well as personal pluses to that summer tour for Gary Chapman. He had never spent so much time in front of an audience, except as a member of someone else's band.

"The tour with Amy was the first time I'd ever been out as a solo artist," he says. "I had a twenty-five-minute warmup act and the whole experience was a blast."

Amy's blossoming attraction to Gary was the fruition of Chapman's battle for her affections. She has described falling in love as a process of elimination.

"My personal feeling on love is, if you're with somebody long enough and have an inclination toward one another, chances are you'll fall in love," Amy says. "I know there are people who meet for the first time and fall in love. A lot of the times it comes from being stuck in a situation."

It's hardly the height of romanticism, unlike Chapman's confession of love at first sight, but one might expect it to be emotionally safer. It was not.

The Grant family thought Chapman was simply a friend with platonic intentions toward their youngest daughter. Amy describes his approach as sneaky, but when the feeling was unconsciously returned by Amy, at least one member of the family took note. When Dan Harrell, brother-in-law, manager, and sometimes surrogate father, found out about their incipient love, he quickly took steps to bring it under his own scrutiny. If they wanted to be boyfriend and girl-friend it would have to be in Nashville, away from any appearance of impropriety on the concert trail. Chapman was fired from the tour after only a few months because of Harrell's injunction against mixing business and pleasure. As long as their personal lives were meshed, their professional lives would be separate.

Her manager's disapproval aside, Amy was dissatisfied with a bickering turn the relationship was taking. Both are strongheaded and neither was likely to bend to the other's opinion on some important matters, which included the influence that Harrell had over Amy's personal as well as professional life.

"We were two young kids trying to figure out who we were and there was this other person complicating things," Amy explains.

With the firing of Gary Chapman came a split in their romance as well. It would be nearly a year before they really got back on truly friendly terms.

"The summer came to an end and I was missing him already and we hadn't even quit the tour," Amy sadly confesses.

The summer of 1980 closed on one tired and unhappy Amy Grant. She was getting worn out from the grind of school, touring, and recording. Amy must have had some doubts whether gospel singing was what she wanted for her life, otherwise she would have had even greater resistance to the stress that achieving the goal entailed. But she was ambivalent about fame.

She harbored the strongly held but nebulous idea that she wanted to be like her mother, to raise a family of four or five children after she finished college. But Amy's big breakthrough was nearly capped by a big breakdown. At odds with her image in the contemporary Christian press, overworked and feeling hemmed in by other people's conceptions of what she should be like as a "professional Christian," Amy decided to leave school for a while at the end of her second year at Furman. She moved back to Nashville to work at the Koinonia bookstore and coffeehouse.

When she embarked upon her sabbatical semester in Nashville, she was comforted to be back in the place where she had first performed. She was once again hanging out near the Belmont Church, near her fatherly and encouraging spiritual mentor, Don Finto. It felt good to be away from the excessive demands she felt her fans made upon her to live up to their image of her.

"I get tired of Christians trying to tell me what being a Christian is," Amy said when she was twenty years old. "I get tired of that kind of Christianity. I don't mean that in a disrespectful way, but it's especially true in the college-age group. People asking, 'Have you had your quiet time today?' We have such a regimented idea of what Christianity is. In college, everybody wears the same thing and they want their walk with the Lord to be the same way. Sometimes I just want to scream, 'I had a loud time with the Lord this morning!' Sometimes I just feel like Christians are boxing themselves in."

With all the changes in her life, it was comforting to again have the friendly and spiritually motivating pastor right next door. Little had changed at the Belmont Church, except that it finally dropped the "Church of Christ" name from the sign out front because its developing doctrine had ranged far afield from that body's espoused beliefs.

More and more young people were joining the congregation all the time. They came not only from Pastor Finto's former base at David Lipscomb College, but from the many colleges and universities within a mile of the church: Vanderbilt University, Peabody College, Scarritt College

(Methodist), and Belmont College (Baptist). The church attracted a contingent of "street people," the barefoot and blue-jeans people. There was an apparent Christian revolution going on among college-aged people, although one not as homogeneous in its dress code and value system as the sixties youth rebellion.

"The first couple of times I visited the church it was packed," Amy recalls. "One of the things I noticed was that a lot of people weren't dressed up—there were a lot of jeans, a lot of bare feet. You felt like the people came to hear what was happening there."

Don Finto attracted tremendous numbers of young people with his message of spiritual rebirth and social outreach. They ranged from the comfortable college crowd to the poor residents of what was in the mid-seventies primarily a near-ghetto behind the Belmont Church. Eventually, all four Grant girls became members. Also drawn into the fold, at first by their daughters' invitation, were Dr. and Mrs. Grant. Finto's personal charm and gentle persuasion led a movement that became something less than a full-blown Charismatic congregation, and yet, while firmly drawing on the basis of Church of Christ teachings, it was quite outside the mainstream of the Church of Christ. Finto had been frozen out of the lecturing and publishing network of Church of Christ orthodoxy because of his emphasis on what he calls a Spirit-filled ministry.

"We were really pursuing the ministry of the Holy Spirit, what He is doing today and how we could be a part of it," Finto explains. "That was in the time period when there were many—hundreds—of young people coming. The whole church, the median age was probably twenty and sometimes you felt like it was eighteen."

Pastor Finto recalls one particular incident from about the same time that Amy was drawn into the Belmont fellowship. His recollection illuminates how the church grew as a center of contemporary Christian music to which Amy could retreat.

"A guy came here from California, a guy who had been bankrupt a couple of times, Gary Paxton," Finto says. "He was living with a common-law wife somewhere here in the neighborhood and was really buying Salvation Army clothes, driving an old clunker, and trying to get his feet on the ground again. He was an alcoholic, dope addict, and various other things."

Paxton had been the leader of an early-sixties pop group called the Hollywood Argyles. The group had only one big hit, but that one was a huge success: "Alley Oop."

"As he told me, when he would get 'good and drunk,' he would read the Bible, because he had some Christian background. But he had never become a Christian. So he and his girlfriend started looking around for a church to go to. Every time they would drive up outside a church they would see the people going in, they felt like they couldn't fit in because they didn't have the clothes to wear.

"One night they were going to the drugstore that used to be across the street. They looked at all the people going in. There were blacks, Orientals, and there were some street people, students, and some older people. Then he saw a couple of people in tuxedos and evening dresses. I thought at first that he had made that up, but it turned out there really were two couples. In fact, Amy Grant's dad and mother was one of them. They were going to something at the country club and came to church first.

"So he and his girlfriend came and I think maybe a month later he gave his life to the Lord, then started writing Christian lyrics."

Paxton, wasted and disillusioned, found a new focus and caught on to the rhythm of contemporary Christian music right away. He founded a contemporary Christian record company called Newpax Records and won a 1976 GMA Dove Award for Album of the Year in the Contemporary

Category for his production with Bob McKenzie of the album "No Shortage" by the Imperials. He is also credited with bringing contemporary Christian artist Don Francisco from obscurity into the Nashville community of gospel pop/rockers.

That former drug store from which Paxton watched people file into the Belmont Church has since become a storefront clothing ministry of that Christian assembly. The adjoining building running down Grand Avenue behind it has become a Bible study resource center for the community-oriented congregation. Mostly through large private donations, Belmont Church has bought and refurbished most of the commercial buildings on the corners of Grand Avenue and Sixteenth Avenue South where the church sits.

The Belmont Church's plain little sanctuary and nearby outreach ministries were an important new center of talent that was to become as influential as it was prolific. The Southeast, still the home ground of traditional gospel music, became, in the late seventies, the last region of America to catch on to contemporary Christian musical styles. Song publishers in Nashville like Paragon, Meadowgreen, and Word had begun putting writers on retainer, providing the economic basis for this growing talent pool.

But these publishers did not put their money on the line just because they felt the spirit move them. During the late seventies and early eighties, a generation of young people, students, and young marrieds, who had been raised listening to rock and pop radio, were finding contemporary Christian music in ever increasing numbers. They were being accompanied in some instances by secular stars who also experienced religious conversion at that time.

B. J. Thomas suffered greatly in the early days of the pop-star transition to the ranks of contemporary Christian music. He was booed, heckled, and spat upon by fundamentalist Christians and for a time lost a lot of his secular fans for mixing pop hits like "Raindrops Keep Falling on My Head" with gospel tunes like "Mighty Clouds of Joy." Still, he persisted.

John Michael Talbot left the seventies country-rock band Mason Proffit and joined a Franciscan order in 1980. Dressed in long plain robes, sandals on his feet, his hair trimmed neatly according to the practices of his order, Talbot began turning out some very intense and mystical worship music. A year earlier, Anaheim Convention Center had hosted a musical event called Hosanna USA, which included performances by such secular-turned-Christian artists as Leon Patillo (formerly with Santana) and Denny Correll (formerly with Blues Image). A pop star for two decades already, Dionne Warwick spoke of her Christian faith openly on national television as she accepted her award at the 1980 Grammy Awards Show. Erotic-pop singer Donna Summer became a Christian, modified her sexual moanings on record and began putting "message music" in between her disco tracks.

By far the most celebrated and controversial of the secular artists whose late-seventies public conversion and correspondent music shifts paved the way for Amy Grant's success was Bob Dylan. If Dylan's folk-song fans had initially objected to his artistic shift from acoustic protest songs to electric rock and country stylings in the late sixties and early seventies, they were flabbergasted when the single "Gotta Serve Somebody" announced his conversion from Judaism to Jesus in 1979.

While Amy was slowly honing her stage presence two weekends out of the month, Dylan was shocking the rock world with the first of three Christian-flavored albums, "Slow Train Coming." A book titled "Dylan—What Happened" was rushed to press following his late-1979 tour in support of the record. Whether or not Dylan's music ever converted anyone to his new religious faith, the record put the issue of Christianity's place in popular music on the front burner of public discussion. Powered by the dynamic single, "Gotta Serve Somebody," "Slow Train Coming" was of significant artistic merit. Dylan set a new high standard for "Christian rock" records, and won the 1980 GMA Dove for Gospel Album of the Year by a Secular Artist for his trouble.

It would be a few years before Amy would invade Dylan's rock stronghold and carry off her own Grammy Award. When Amy left Furman, she spent most of her time at the original outreach storefront of the Belmont Church, the Koinonia bookstore and coffeehouse.

During that fall/winter nonsemester, Amy occasionally saw Gary Chapman. They sometimes met at the Koinonia. The coffeehouse side of Koinonia features sand-blasted, red brick walls and gray-blue ceiling, with a kitchenette near the small stage in the back where refreshments are prepared for music night attendees. A safe crowd would not exceed fifty patrons, and there were few writer's nights in the winter of 1980–81 drawing that many. Amy saw thousands more people during her summer and autumn tours, which included dates on the Billy Graham Crusade and as an opening act for the well-established Bill Gaither Trio.

Blanton and Harrell dropped Dharma Agency to handle Amy's tour scheduling in-house. This happened, in part, because Gaither's Springhouse Productions tour-packaging company wanted to book a big block of Amy's available dates for their own shows. Springhouse also was instrumental in arranging dates for Amy's first big tour, which took place in early 1981, backed by the contemporary Christian rock band of gospel duo Ed DeGarmo and Dana Key. The tour would be a boost for both Amy Grant and DeGarmo and Key.

"She was the darling of the gospel industry at that time and they were the outcasts," explains Dan Brock, DeGarmo and Key's manager/booking agent. "We got a lot of bad press from the gospel establishment people who said they were ruining Amy's music by playing it too loud, but at the time she was drawing a couple of thousand people and we were only drawing about four hundred or five hundred, so it gave us a lot of exposure. It was also more luxurious than we'd done before. Ed and Dana and the boys had been traveling around in this little van we had and on this tour we got to ride on their buses."

The touring relationship between the struggling band and Amy Grant resulted in a vocal collaboration among Amy, DeGarmo, and Key. The tune "Nobody Loves Me Like You Do" (not the Anne Murray/Dave Loggins duet hit of the same title) appeared on Amy's concert LP and on the DeGarmo and Key album "This Ain't Hollywood" in separate live and studio versions.

Just before that tour got under way, Amy registered for classes at Vanderbilt University in Nashville to make her touring and recording easier. Vanderbilt is a bastion of Southern upper-class socialization and education, with a reputation for both scholastic quality and a pervasive fraternity and sorority social life. Vanderbilt had cast off its church affiliation in the early part of this century, separating itself from Southern Methodism, but the university is still the home of a large ecumenical Divinity School. Don Finto earned his doctor of philosophy degree there.

Amy moved into a dormitory and joined her sister Carol's sorority, Kappa Alpha Theta. She managed to find time that semester and in the summer of 1981 to do about forty dates with DeGarmo and Key, improving her act and making the move to a harder rock sound. The first few dates on that tour through the Southwest in February 1981, were especially memorable. They were recorded by a mobile sound truck and became her twin record releases for that year, "Amy Grant—In Concert" and "In Concert, Vol. II."

Amy's abilities as an instrumentalist had developed to the point where she played her guitar on the live album sets, a first for her on a record. She felt she was becoming better accepted by the contemporary Christian musicians in Nashville. Her feelings that they had derided her capabilities since she arrived on the scene at seventeen had contributed to her identity crisis and an insecurity about her talents. That feeling would continue to crop up from time to time. Fronting the accomplished band of Ed DeGarmo and Dana Key in 1981 enabled her to step closer to a mainstream rock style and established her as a viable "big show" act.

"I felt that initially I was really accepted and well received by the audiences, but among the music people I was really looked down upon," she recalls. "They were all thinking . . . all the young kids buy [her records] because she sings so simply. They all thought that the three-year-old kid next door could write my songs. But that's just it; the three-year-old next door was not writing them."

Replacing Gary Chapman, on tours with Amy and the band, was guitarist/singer/songwriter Billy Sprague. Though Sprague, too, became something of a constant companion to Amy Grant, he did not replace Gary Chapman in her heart, or as a musical influence in her career.

Chapman's contributions to her music had been steadily growing. "Father's Eyes" helped Amy Grant's music tap a growing trend in contemporary Christian music that began in the late seventies. There was a sensibility in his music that agreed with the image Amy's managerial team wanted her to project, even if they didn't particularly want Gary hanging around with her on the road. Chapman landed credits for five of twelve songs on Amy's 1980 Word Records release, "Never Alone." Two of those tunes featured Gary and Amy as coauthors. The titles of their coauthored songs, "Walking Away with You" (written with Chris Christian) and "Don't Give Up on Me" (written with Brown Bannister), seem to describe their on-again, off-again relationship.

"Gary was early," explains Randy Cox, Meadowgreen

Music general manager who brought Chapman over from Paragon. "Most people [in the late seventies] were not writing lyrics with the depth that he was doing. But with those songs, I believe, Gary came in where the music had maybe been written but the words weren't finished, or maybe both, and he'd finish them. He's really good at that —he's a song doctor, but I think he's really better when he writes his own songs."

Chapman's career had been boosted by Amy's cuts, as well as tunes recorded by such gospel artists as Doug Oldham, Jamie Owens-Collins, the Cruise Family, the Blackwood Brothers, and Rusty Goodman. It was at about this time that Randy Cox and Gary Chapman left Paragon for Meadowgreen. Paragon had merged with gospel publishing giant the Benson Company in 1980, holding Cox over until he resigned in early 1981 to head the fledgling Meadowgreen Music company.

"It all happened real quick then," Cox says. "Gary was my first signee [at Meadowgreen]. A week later he was named GMA Songwriter of the Year, then we laid down the first demo of 'Finally.'"

"Father's Eyes" and the Jamie Owens-Collins hit "I'm Yours Lord" helped him beat the odds as the new boy among five finalists for the Dove Best Composer Award that winter. After three years of nominations, he proudly mounted the stage at the Tennessee Performing Arts Center to accept his trophy as Songwriter of the Year. Chapman was suddenly in the spotlight from all directions, but he was not the only musician or songwriter involved with Amy Grant in 1981 to receive honors. Both "Father's Eyes" and "I'm Yours Lord" were beat out for Song of the Year honors by the praise tune "Praise The Lord" which was written by Amy's producer Brown Bannister and Mike Hudson.

The Bannister/Hudson win with "Praise The Lord," from their duo album of the same title, took nothing away from Chapman's strength as a writer, but amplified a GMA

membership preference for unambiguous praise and worship music even in the contemporary Christian camp. It
also reflected Bannister's own rise as a songwriter, producer, and sometime artist. He increasingly developed a
sound in the studio that was distinctively his own. Bannister's success as a producer has not been limited to Amy
Grant records, or even to his own rare efforts.

In 1980, Brown Bannister was enlisted to produce an
album by Debby Boone, daughter of the original "clean
teen," Pat Boone. The elder Boone, who continues to be a
force in family and Christian entertainment, was also a
product of an earlier generation of Nashville and Church of
Christ influences. Boone attended the church's David Lipscomb College in Nashville before embarking on a recording and film career that was marked by adherence to his
own strict, church-derived values in the selection of songs
and de-emphasis on love scenes in his movies.

For Debby Boone's album, "With My Song," Bannister
picked a tune called "Sing," from an album by the Pennsyl-
vania-based contemporary Christian band Glad. The album came out on her father's gospel label, Lamb & Lion
Records. Debby Boone's record earned Bannister his second Dove Award in 1981 when it took honors as Gospel
Album of the Year by a Secular Artist. "Sing," from that
album, also served as a harbinger of contemporary-fla-
vored praise music, a trend that Bannister would continue
with Amy Grant thereafter.

For Chapman, in 1982, the world was full of opportunity.
Meadowgreen backed him with a wealth of financial and
administrative resources, as well as the publishing experience of Randy Cox and the clout and connections of country music publishing giant Tree International. The GMA
Award gave him tremendous notoriety almost overnight.
He had also gained valuable exposure and stage experience
as his own man in front of Amy's fans.

"The Lord allowed me to be out in front of a ready-made

audience and I was very grateful for the opportunity," Chapman thankfully recalls.

Of course, his instant notoriety didn't necessarily follow with instant riches. Chapman was still sharing a house in Nashville with three friends and playing guitar on the occasional recording session to make ends meet. With all his success, he still described himself as a struggling songwriter.

Without a full-time boyfriend that semester, Amy turned to her sorority sisters at Vanderbilt, when she wasn't touring with DeGarmo and Key, and began to meet more people on campus. She found the atmosphere at Vanderbilt vastly more stimulating than the previous years at Furman. At Vanderbilt she was not regarded as an oddity for being a youngster on the go.

"Everyone at Vanderbilt seems to be an achiever," Amy says. "Everybody's out there doing something."

Amy found most of the students she met there had a broad base of experience. They had traveled, read widely, perhaps even worked at summer jobs that gave them a sharp focus on their career goals early in college. There is a great sense of confidence among Vanderbilt undergraduates, and a common expectation of accomplishment in the social and business world that lay beyond the campus confines.

Vanderbilt is a conservative institution, one that attracts studious, yet fun-loving undergraduates who are generally politically conservative. According to the student-written assessment of the Vanderbilt student body published in the 1980–81 yearbook, "The mood on campus after Reagan's election seemed to be one of nearly uniform satisfaction." Although Amy's social background—her family is part of the professional class of the Southern gentry—gave her plenty of values and ideas in common with her classmates, Amy found herself somewhat socially out of place. For despite her sorority affiliation, and Kappa Alpha Theta was one of the biggest on campus that year, Amy discovered the flip side to her first encounter with her gospel-singing peers at the GMA Awards, which had given her feelings of being an outsider. If she wasn't like the girls who'd been raised inside the family mold of the traditional gospel business, she was also different from "civilians." She found that singing of her faith stigmatized her in some of the university's hard-partying circles.

"Sometimes I think it's a little unrealistic to think the only thoughts a person has are Christian thoughts," Amy recalls. "I remember going to a fraternity party and you just sense the electricity starting to happen. Some guy's paying you some attention and then somebody goes, 'Hey, this is the gospel singer' and *phhht,* there it goes. I felt like saying, 'Hey, look, I can flirt, I can date, I will kiss good night, we can embrace.' But once the stereotype is there—wham!"

Amy's life-style message to her fans, which adolescent girls find particularly attractive, is her insistence that it is all right to be sexy and Christian. Amy refuses to accept limitations on being what she calls a "vibrant and alive" Christian woman. She has searched the pages of the New Testament and found nothing that says a girl can't be wholesome, moral, and have sex appeal at the same time. On the contrary, in reading her Old Testament, Amy has found many examples of the earthiness and sensuality of the Hebrew matriarchs.

"It kind of makes you look at what we've elevated as being godly," Amy told one of Nashville's foremost music journalists, Robert K. Oermann. "Quite honestly, what we consider godly and what is scripturally godly are diverse sometimes. Because, I mean, historically the women in the Bible were just unbelievable women. In the Old Testament they were some of the most charismatic, magnetic, daring, risking women—beautiful, sexual. Part of the Puritan philosophy was neuter. Then there was Shakertown [a nineteenth-century socioreligious experiment in which men and women lived communal, but celebate, lives]. I never read any descriptions of anything like that in the Bible."

Many Vanderbilt boys were intimidated by her status as a "professional Christian." They avoided Amy in any normal social situation. "They think you're a female Billy Graham with a guitar," she complained. She must have experienced more than a little frustration in her social life by the time the end of that school year rolled around.

In May of that year, Amy ran into Gary at a movie theater. Gary held back. He felt somewhat brushed off from the past year's firing and subsequent breakup. Amy felt a tug at her heart that she wouldn't admit to herself, but it was obviously going to be up to her to start communication between them again. She walked over to Chapman and broke the ice. Would he mind talking to her about what had happened between them?

"That night we realized that even if we couldn't work out anything else, our friendship was too valuable to give up," Amy confessed.

Everyone gets bearded in the Word Records annual picnic and pie-eating contest (l–r) Bobby Apone, Eric Wyse, and Amy Grant.

Photo by Alan Mayor

Santa didn't have to ask if this little girl had been good—sales of
her record "Age to Age" were certified over the half-million mark
a few weeks later and Amy got an RIAA gold record by Christmas
that year.

Photo by Don Foster

There was a lot of pride taken in the haul of GMA Dove Awards that fateful night in April 1983 when Amy won three Doves, including the honor as Gospel Artist of the Year.

Photo by Bill Thorup

It's all in the family, though more Dove Awards went home with
Sandi Patti's family than Amy Grant's in 1984. l–r: Dana Key,
Greg Nelson, Sandi Patti, John Helvering (Patti's husband),
David Clydesdale, Amy Grant, Ed DeGarmo.

Onstage teamwork rounds out Amy and Gary's lives together.

Photo by Larry Dixon

Amy shares the spotlight with pianist Michael W. Smith during her Straight Ahead Tour.

"Here's my family," quips Amy as husband Gary carries their pet dog on stage to take a bow.   Photo by Alan Mayor

Vol Jam host Charlie Daniels joins Amy in a country-gospel duet.
The annual event is Nashville's favorite rock 'n' roll homecoming
party and is broadcast via Voice of America to millions of listeners around the world.   Photo by Larry Dixon

Chapter 9

As Amy and Gary reignited the flame of their friendship, both had new albums entering the expanding contemporary Christian music market. Chapman's first Lamb & Lion release, "Sincerely Yours," was his debut as a Christian recording artist. Amy's winter tour had gotten under way the previous February with live recordings at Oral Roberts University Mabee Center auditorium in Tulsa. It bore its first fruit with "Amy Grant—In Concert." Key figures in both projects were the Memphis-based duo, Ed DeGarmo and Dana Key. They provided the musical backup for Amy's two-volume set of live albums, while they jointly produced "Sincerely Yours" with Jo Hardy, for Blanton/Harrell Productions, at their own Ardent Recording studios in Memphis.

The DeGarmo and Key band that backed Amy included Mike Brignardello on bass, Gregg Morrow at drums, and Gerry Peters playing Oberheim synthesizer. Ed DeGarmo played keyboard while Dana Key played electric guitar. Billy Sprague, a developing artist in the growing Blanton and Harrell stable, played acoustic guitar and helped a four-person backup vocal group fill in behind Amy. Most of the songs on her first live album came from her previous records. However, one new tune came from Amy's own pen

—an inclusion that acquired extra poignancy by the time it was released.

Amy was not yet six when her great grandfather, A. M. Burton, died in 1966. His widow, Mrs. Lilly May Burton, loved her great grandchildren and grandchildren and seemed to especially like having them play around her 109-acre farm, just outside of the eastern corner of Belle Meade. When Dr. Grant moved his family back to Tennessee, he bought a house very near the southerly boundaries of the Burton estate. As Nashville's population grew, so did the housing density of Green Hills, until Burton Farm represented one of the largest solid tracts of undeveloped land in that part of Davidson County. Mrs. Burton no longer actually owned the land, due to her late husband's life estate bequest to David Lipscomb College, but still dwelled there in the fine, old house. Great grandmother Burton's rocking chairs, fireplace, and squeaky farmhouse stairs created many dear images in Amy's memory.

Amy wrote a song about her great grandmother, whom she called Mimi, and sang it on the DeGarmo and Key tour. The song, called "Mimi's House," is as touching a tribute to a grandparent as Gail Davies's classic "Grandma's Song," which made the country Top Ten the same year. "Mimi" Burton died before the album was completed and never got to hear her famous great grandchild's sweet testimonial to her laughter and warmth.

Even though Amy's star was obviously on the rise, she still suffered moments of wistful self-doubt. "I'll never be a star," Amy penned from Los Angeles in a postcard to a friend that year. She was in the West Coast music capital to attend the National Academy of Recording Arts and Sciences Grammy presentations. She was nominated in a gospel music category, but must have sensed it was not yet her year to win.

> "I'll never be a star,
> I just prefer to wish upon them,

Greet them at dusk,
And watch them fall."

That's how the postcard poem read. The message comes
from her heart, a young woman's rejection of the Hollywood star-making machinery and its counterpart in the
gospel music industry. Recognition of her in the world of
professional entertainment was growing each month, as the
Grammy nomination and the GMA Dove Award nominations of the two previous years attested. The legion of Amy
Grant fans continued to grow.

Yet Amy writing that delicate metaphor of nature asserts
a sentiment that was pervasive throughout her career-
building years. It was a mixture of modesty, humility, and
just plain self-protective denial—for nothing hurts the ego
worse than the loss of fame when one depends upon it too
much for one's self-esteem and identity.

"I don't really care to ever be a star," Amy told Nashville
Banner reporter Michael Erickson. "Maybe it's because
I feel like I've experienced enough recognition to
know . . ."

The Grammy would evade her grasp at the 1982 ceremonies, but recognition followed her at Vanderbilt.

"I guess I don't really have my finger on the pulse of my
recognition," she confessed as a Vanderbilt coed. "I feel
like to the Christian community I'm basically known. But, if
I happen to be in somebody's class and ask a lot of dumb
questions, I'm sure that's the way they would know me—
'the girl who asks the dumb questions.' "

Her dumb questions may have come from gaps in her
attendance at college lectures. Touring kept her from at-
taining perfect attendance in the classroom, but she managed to integrate into her own social circle at Vanderbilt.
Amy lived on campus, shared a dormitory suite with several
other girls, and was as active as her career demands would
let her be in Theta sorority activities. In that way, Vander-

bilt was the place where she could be her real self. She was among bright, outgoing, and motivated college kids just like herself. Talking girl-to-girl with her roommates and sorority sisters, late-night bull sessions over soft drinks and pizzas refreshed her between all-night recording sessions, long weekend concert trips, and vacation tours.

"I couldn't hold up a facade if I wanted to," she explained. "There are six of us in my dorm suite. I'm in a sorority. I know those girls, they know me. They know the performer side but they also know just the crazy side and the quiet side."

Amy was also exposed to the wilder side of Vanderbilt campus life. Nearly as well known for its social activities as its excellence in scholarship, Vanderbilt's fraternity and sorority world would have offered her many opportunities to witness the abuses and excesses often found on the party scene. Having learned from the Belmont Church's welcome of people involved in the hell of the drug world and other self-abusive life-styles, Amy feels that tolerance of human frailties is a way of loving without condoning things she regards as wrong. She would take her observations, plus the memory of her own Harpeth Hall Winterim trip to England during her senior year, and incorporate them into her message. She encourages her young fans to choose the godly way through their own informed free will.

"I don't want to encourage undiscerning youth," Amy says. "They need to understand the world. Total abstension is not the way. Some kids never learn to handle the world when they are away from the family or a protected Christian environment. You can't insulate yourself with only believers. My mom and dad felt Jesus needed to be real for me wherever I was. There has to be a point where children go through it.

"I saw all the temptations—drugs, etc., but the relaxed atmosphere makes you make the decision face-to-face with the problem. If you are in a regimented situation, you aren't making the decision. Too often, Jesus can become associated with the bureaucracy of the school to some kids. That's not the way it should be because then He becomes the focus of rebellion, not the school."

In 1981, Amy and Brown Bannister undertook a crucial project together. It would be the first of a series of giant steps to move Amy to the forefront of contemporary Christian music—and would be so successful that for the next several years her name would be the only link for people outside the gospel music subculture when they heard the term "contemporary Christian music."

Mike Blanton and Bannister reviewed material and discussed with Dan Harrell the concept for Amy's most praise-oriented album effort to date, "Age to Age." Though they could only hope in the beginning, "Age to Age" would blast her to the top of the class of young contemporary Christian artists. It would establish her as not only one of the darlings of contemporary gospel, but as the hottest-selling act in all of gospel music. And this time she would have Gary Chapman's close support all the way.

As Amy moved through the summer of that year, she and Gary became quite serious about each other. During her younger teens, Amy used to pray for the Lord to send her a husband, and it must have appeared to her ever increasingly that summer that perhaps He was doing so at last. After Amy and Gary's meeting at the movie, they defused the heavy boyfriend/girlfriend roles they'd suffered under previously. With no expectations, their feelings for each other blossomed.

They drove through the beautiful rural countryside, especially south of the city beyond the Burton Farm toward Franklin, which was full of historic Civil War–era mansions and farmsteads. They took guitars, sang together, and dreamed of someday owning one of the fine old homesteads hidden among the gently rolling green hills and slow-moving streams that feed the Harpeth River.

"That took the pressure off," Amy says. "That September he asked me to marry him."

Aside from the obvious stimulation which people with extraordinary talent derive from each other's company, Amy found more to love than Chapman's sincerity and sense of humor.

"One of the first things that attracted me to my husband was, I mean he'll probably never be on the cover of *GQ* [*Gentlemen's Quarterly* magazine], but he . . . you just get the feeling that you think you're walking through the threshold of his personality," Amy tries to explain. "You see one hundred more doors in front of you. It doesn't stop with how many weights you can lift. It doesn't even stop with what your feelings are about life. I mean, you go past the emotion, you go past the soul, and suddenly there's a person that's approached the spiritual realm with arms open and saying as deep as I can, 'Go in this life—I want to understand.' That's the only way I can describe it to myself. It's almost like a magnet that pulls so much deeper than the surface."

Living at Vanderbilt at summer's end, 1981, Amy was now closer to her recording sessions, but her tours and the stepped-up recording work drew her away from school-work and classes more than ever. Often, she carried her portable electric typewriter along on the bus when she went out on the concert trail. Term papers had to be written on the run, to the grinding rhythm of the monotonous diesel bus engines and the huge rubber tires biting off mile after mile of highway. She would soon have to decide which was more important—school or singing.

For the time being, Amy enjoyed the challenge and stimulation of a college campus she was able to really be a part of, if only because she no longer had to catch airplanes to get from her last class on Friday afternoon to her first recording session of the weekend.

In the fall of 1981, Amy started back to school on an

ecstatic note. She was engaged to an incredibly talented, witty, and caring young man only three years her senior— and she was recording tunes for her next album, "Age to Age." There were soul-stirring rousers like "Sing Your Praise to the Lord," which had come from Richard Mullins, a writer who, like Gary Chapman, was on the roster at the yearling Meadowgreen Music arm of Tree International. There were, of course, more collaborative tunes between Amy, Gary, and various others, and a couple of new writers, piano whiz Michael W. Smith and New York "heart singer" Kathy Troccoli. Troccoli had been pried from the protective arms of her family by Dan Harrell, who promised to take the youngster into his own home at first and treat her just like part of his own family.

Most importantly, for the music and for the impact on the gospel music world, there was a tune by Michael Card and John Thompson called "El Shaddai." Card's music, especially, is much richer than either Amy's or Gary's, with themes of worship and praise. Tunes from Amy's pen could be fun vaudeville-type vamps like "Fat Baby" or the humorous "Grape, Grape Joy" from her first album. She typically wrote her lyrics around topics like "don't give up on me, Lord" or "look what faith is doing in my life," essential questions for her young audience to grapple with, but not as heavily scriptural as the traditionalists in the gospel field really liked best. Card and Thompson hit both the young contemporary Christians and the older gospel traditionalists close to the heart with their magnificent, soaring melody.

Amy turned in perhaps her finest vocal delivery when she powered home the tune's scripture-based lyrics. "El Shaddai" borrowed words from the Old Testament Hebrew to call God's name (El Shaddai means God Almighty) and issued two other key Hebraic chants of praise. With that song she stepped forward from the ranks of teen phenomenon to showcase a maturing talent to which the whole industry would soon pay tribute.

Amy and Gary postponed immediate plans for marriage, leaving nearly a year from the time Amy accepted his proposal that September. They also put off ultimate gratification of their desire for each other. Sexual control, in this instance, may be Amy's most prominent moral badge as far as being a role model for her teenaged fans. It is not something she brags about, but simply a choice she made and found the strength to stick with. Primarily she uses anecdotes about her failings in life and faith to encourage people to forgive themselves and not let giving in to a particular "sin" (still a missing word in her musical lexicon) keep one from continuing to seek God.

"I made a conscious effort to say, 'I am going to save the most intimate part for the person I spend the rest of my life with,'" she said.

"I was twenty-one when we married and I said to Gary, 'Man, that was tough. There were a lot of guys I deeply loved and would have enjoyed knowing fully, man-to-woman, woman-to-man, but I persevered so that I could give myself to you.

"People say, 'Prude, prude, prude,' but I'm glad I didn't cross certain barriers, because I wouldn't want to compare Gary's moans with some other guy's."

Chapman, three years her senior and generally a more rollicking person, had not been so stalwart.

"Sure, it bothered me a little that he did not wait for me, too," she said with a smirk. "But he has said if he could undo anything about his growing up, it would have been to know only one woman—me."

If young adults among her fans are tempted to measure themselves against the standards of sexual behavior Amy set for herself, Amy stresses that her virginity was a personal choice. She places no onus on those who choose the more pervasive social more of trying premarital sex.

"I have friends who did cross those barriers and don't seem to be the worse for wear," she said. "They continue to love and honor each other."

None of which means that Amy doesn't enjoy feeling sexy—but she insists on defining that word and feeling, as she does most of her opinions, in the context of her Christian faith.

"What is 'sexy'?" she asks. "To me it has never been taking off my shirt or having my tongue sticking out. I feel that a Christian young woman in the eighties is very sexual."

In September of 1981, Amy registered for more literature classes and a couple of music courses at Blair School of Music at Vanderbilt. She knuckled down to a busy semester at the beginning of what should have been her last year of college.

The demands of school were made all the more difficult that fall by Amy's recording and touring schedule, which was becoming more keen. The Blanton/Harrell plan of using their strong financial base to wait out the growing demand was paying off, but demand had grown so great that it could neither be sated with her limited number of weekends and holidays nor put off much longer. There comes a time in each vineyard when the grapes must be harvested.

Spring semester at Vanderbilt was just too busy for her. Among the courses she failed for missing too many class sessions while on tour was a piano studio course. She was attempting to build upon her childhood music lessons and her ability to sight-read musical notes—a knowledge she acquired to sing in the Church of Christ where there was no organ or piano leading the melody for hymns.

"[In church] I stood next to Kathy, who's eight years older than me, and she told me, 'There are notes on the page,' " Amy recalls. "If I wanted to sing with the rest, I should learn them out and follow them. By about fourth grade everybody knew how to read music a little."

It didn't help her now, however. The spirit can be willing, but if the body is on a bus somewhere between Tallahassee and Tennessee when the roll is called in class, that's all that counts in the grade book.

Failure in school would leave her still twenty credit hours shy of graduation. Her picture would not appear in the Vanderbilt yearbook among the graduating seniors. Of course, none of them got a full-page portrait and article about themselves in the 1982 *Commodore,* Vanderbilt's yearbook, like she did, either. That seems to have symbolically summed up the direction Amy's life was taking.

The choice loomed: music or school.

"It got so insane trying to go to school and we had a three-and-a-half-week tour right in the middle," Amy says. "So at Vanderbilt I really bombed. I had several mandatory attendance classes and I got an automatic 'F.' I didn't realize they were mandatory attendance until it was too late to drop them.

"I was living the life of two people. It became a no-win situation. I plan to go back sometime."

With her marriage set for early that summer, she knew she wouldn't be in any frame of mind for the grind of summer school and heavy touring. No, as quickly as things were happening for her, marriage would offer the perfect opportunity to take a much-needed break from everything. She could then come back to put all her best efforts into her career.

"I mean, I will sing all my life, but popularity comes and goes," she opines. "Five years from now I might not be able to draw two people to my concerts. It would just seem unfortunate to have the opportunity and only do a halfway job, and that's what I was really doing. I was doing a halfway job at singing and a halfway job with my schoolwork."

The May 1982 issuance of "Age to Age" would be the

beginning to an exciting, accelerating new period in Amy's life and career. Her artistry on record was beginning to mature at last. The unstoppable momentum of her career would push her into the limelight she had so long wished to avoid. She would step into that role as gospel superstar in only a few months, but there was a breathing space for her personal life just weeks away. As that flubbed semester drew to a close, ending her college career unfinished while opening a new and bigger chapter on her musical career, Amy faced the most joyous moment of her personal life— her wedding day.

Chapter 10

In the spring of 1982, plans for the stylish society wedding of Amy Grant and Gary Chapman were in her family's hands. While Gloria Grant saw to the details in fine old Southern style, Chapman was rehearsing a pickup band for the upcoming live recording of his second Lamb & Lion album, "Happenin'." Bassist Mike Brignardello was again loaned by DeGarmo and Key for the album, which they would produce during two shows held in the Tennessee Performing Arts Center in Nashville in late April of 1982. A few weeks later Word Records released "Age to Age." Also joining in what Chapman would style "the Happenin' Band" was keyboard wizard and songwriter Michael W. Smith. Smith's instrumental support role was destined to continue with Gary and Amy for a couple of years until, with help from Blanton and Harrell, he finally launched his own solo career full-time.

Included on "Happenin'" are Gary's version of "Father's Eyes" and "Finally," his two biggest hits as a songwriter. Also included is a moving song of praise called "Treasure," which often reoccurs on Amy Grant tours. Amy joined Gary (less than two months before they were set to walk down the aisle at Vine Street Christian Church) to sing a duet with him—not on "Father's Eyes"—but on a beautiful love ballad, "Always." Among the in-jokes on the album's liner notes was Chapman's tongue-in-cheek assessment of Dan Harrell's managerial style—Chapman tagged him with the nickname "Bulldog." That Gary and Amy would be a "media couple" seems to have been alluded to when he announced her in his credits as "my immediate family."

Belmont Church's Sixteenth Avenue sanctuary is plain and much too small a place in which to hold the wedding of the daughter of an important Belle Meade family. Guest lists for such Nashville society weddings can easily run into the 700–800-person range and Belmont only holds about 400 in a tight squeeze. The church itself has for the last couple of years held Sunday morning services in the tall-ceilinged, two-tier wooden auditorium of West End Junior High to accommodate the nearly 1,500 members coming to worship.

Amy and Gary decided to say their wedding vows on Saturday, June 19, 1982, in front of a huge assemblage of friends, family friends, and church associates at Nashville's Vine Street Christian Church. The Christian Church in the South is one of the three distinct sects that grew out of the Disciples of Christ movement from which the Church of Christ derived. There is something of a natural kinship between the Belmont Church and Vine Street Christian, being different daughters of the same historical religious movement.

The wedding was a formal affair. Don Finto officiated, while Gary's brother, Keith, father T. W. Chapman, and a Texas pal, Dennis Lewis, joined his retinue of groomsmen, which also included Blanton, Harrell, Michael W. Smith, Word Records employee and former roommate Andy Tolbird, publisher Randy Cox, and Jerry Verner.

Amy was a beautiful bride, clothed in a traditionally styled white wedding gown, accentuated by a gold cross pendant that hung around her neck. Her attendants naturally included sisters Mimi, Carol, and Kathy. She also had in attendance Gary's sister Sharry Chapman Kitchell and school friends Jeannie Cochran, Helen Maddox, Leigh Ann Jones, Scottie Fillebrown, and Sloan Tower. The reception was held at the Grant's home on Lynwood Lane, a quiet, hidden cul de sac in Belle Meade. Upon leaving the church in a rented limousine, the new Mr. and Mrs. Chapman announced that they would honeymoon in Banff, Canada. An even better honeymoon trip was actually planned for a little later that summer.

First, though, there were the inevitable adjustments of transition from dating to setting up household together. Gary and Amy bought a multistory condominium comfortably off the main street of Belle Meade's shopping district, located at the edge of the high-priced 37205 zip-code area of her parents' part of town. Some of those adjustments to marital life were especially hard for Amy, who had never lived outside the protective environments of home and dormitory. Chapman, after all, had been out on his own for nearly six years before settling down as a husband.

"It's funny, but during the first couple of months of the marriage I think we kind of lost our friendship," Amy explains. "I did have a lot of adjustments to make. I was the youngest in my family and the most pampered."

And then there was sex. No one tells people with the willpower to wait that "it's only sex," not in and of itself the end-all of experience. It can take on an undue importance by its very denial. In making what, for Amy, was the right moral decision, there was undoubtedly an emotional loading of the unknown, an expectation that all the intimacies of married life, major and minor ones combined, would dramatically and immediately change her life for the better. She was disappointed at first.

"Somewhere deep inside I had a lot of insecurity," Amy says with the honesty that keeps her as vulnerable to a reporter's question as to an audience of ten thousand fans.

"Before we were married, I figured as long as Gary never had me, he'd always want me. We always had to fight so hard to be together. So, when we were finally left alone, there was about a four-month yawn."

"She gets so honest that she forgets the good parts," retorts Chapman.

One of the good parts that followed soon after their wedding day was a five-week tour of Europe. It combined the elements of extended vacation with a chance to play their music for the growing network of European Christian youth festivals.

The trip represented a chance to get away from mounting pressures and restrictions of Amy's rising stardom in America. It was also a welcome break in the tension which she recalls surrounded their adjustment period.

"Gary and I went to Europe for five weeks, playing for room and board anyplace we could get on. It was really interesting, playing in parks and at a lot of youth gatherings. Sometimes we would just go to a music festival and tell the promoter we played music and they would put us on the list. Nobody over there knew us from Adam. It was just wonderful."

They opened a number of shows for Barry McGuire, who has a big following among young people overseas. Tastes in popular and gospel music are somewhat different in the cultural crazy quilt of continental Western Europe than in the United States. Amy and Gary also ran up against a language barrier that provided some comic moments during what Amy has dubbed their "Death Tour."

"It was a very loosely organized tour," Amy recalls. "We sang for our room and board five weeks. We'd been married seven weeks when we left. About halfway through I thought, 'If we make it through this, we can make it through a life together.' In about the first week we talked about everything we knew to talk about. We sat down to dinner and nobody spoke our language. It was like, 'So, who did you vote for in '68?' There was nothing to talk about. So here we were newlyweds, I'm sleeping on an Army cot and he's sleeping somewhere else, the beds are falling in at night.

"Our big thrill was when we sang in a place called Brugg. This is not Bruge, Belgium it's Brugg, Switzerland. We sang at some kind of a ruin, it was like a circle of stones and obviously had pillars. There were about six thousand people there and we were invited to be part of a music festival there. They were cheering when we walked out and at first they told us do six or seven songs, but by the time we got up it was only two songs. We were the nobodies so they cut us way down. We got a standing ovation so we did one more song. We walked off and said, 'This will be incredible, the record company will be so excited. We've spread our names and spread our music.'

"We walked off and someone came up to shake our hands and they said, 'Now what is your name?' We said Gary Chapman and Amy Grant. They said, 'They didn't introduce you, they just said here's the two Americans.'"

When "the two Americans" finally came home to Nashville, one of them was fast becoming a superstar. Led by the powerful single, "El Shaddai," Amy's album "Age to Age" rolled up sales of two hundred thousand units in short order. Such unit sales are respectable for a pop act, more than respectable in country music circles, and, at that time, were practically unheard of for a gospel act. Of course, the traditional family acts and Southern vocal quartets sold uncounted millions of albums off the stage and from the back of the bus during their careers. But none of them had sold nearly a quarter of a million copies of a brand new album in the first few months through regular retail outlets like the Christian Booksellers network of retail stores. The concept of Christian bookstores devoting significant floor space for record racks really grew with the spread of contemporary Christian music through the late seventies and the early eighties.

"Age to Age" had sold to the three-hundred-thousand-unit mark by early spring 1983. Dan Harrell bragged that it was the fastest-selling record in Word's history, that it was being bought off Christian Bookstore racks at the unheard of rate of five thousand to six thousand copies per week. It is those kind of quick sales that denote a major phenomenon. Blanton and Harrell added $20,000 worth of lighting and sound equipment to Amy's tour, expanding her on-stage support group to ten people and providing a ten-man contingent of roadies, lighting technicians, and sound engineers. The tour would probably lose money, but Dan Harrell's plan, as always, was for the long range. The exposure, reception, and experience she received on the Age to Age tour was worth the investment. Later, Word, Inc. released a full-length concert home video, produced by Nashville's Scene Three Productions, that helped recoup the expenses of the tour.

In 1982, Amy-mania was sweeping the marketplace, bringing a host of other record companies into the fray as they had never been in it before. CBS Records, which, like most major labels, had always welcomed religious records into the catalog of their major country stars, such as Johnny Cash and Tennessee Ernie Ford, opened the doors on Priority Records as a fully autonomous, full-service gospel label. The CBS all-gospel wing developed as the secular record companies began to sense big money in growing gospel markets. Priority signed up such contemporary Christian acts as Carmen and Cynthia Clawson, took large and expensively appointed office space on Nashville's prestigious West End Avenue, and began treating a full range of gospel music with all the commercial marketing push of a secular label, just as Blanton and Harrell and Word Record's young vice president Stan Moser had been doing successfully with Amy Grant.

MCA Records reopened its old Songbird gospel sublabel with California offices, and began pumping out well-produced efforts by the likes of B. J. Thomas, Dan Peak (former member of the rock trio America), Mylon LeFevre, and Fireworks. Benson Company expanded its roster and built bigger facilities, while Sparrow Records in California also got bigger. Everybody who could do so was plunging in headfirst to catch the rising wave of contemporary Christian music. The secular label efforts in particular suffered from early overspending and a miscalculation about just how quickly the gospel market would grow. By early 1984 Priority and Songbird would be closed down, while many giant gospel labels quietly reduced staff due to a record-industry slump. Nonetheless, sublimely at the top of that wave, unaffected as always by the hoopla, was Amy Grant.

"For some people, it really gives them a lift if they're recognized in an airport," says Amy, who by that time was carrying a six-piece rock band that included Gary Chapman, Michael W. Smith, and three backup singers on her "Age to Age" tour. "That just really doesn't float my boat. It really doesn't *hurt* my day, but it just really doesn't make a difference."

She was increasingly the focus of adulation that matched the kind of hero worship heaped upon pop stars. Teens stopped her on the street or in airports and asked for her autograph. It all caught Amy, who prizes her offstage privacy, quite off guard. That her most ardent fans were primarily well-scrubbed and fashion-conscious girls in their early teens also surprised her at first, though, considering that was her own background, perhaps it should not have. Amy was performing with the same unselfconscious naturalness she always had, singing the songs that told what she believed, more or less oblivious to any conscious plan to appeal to any particular demographic group.

"I remember when I was younger I thought, gee, after a concert when I go talk to the kids they were all girls," Amy says. "And, you know, I wasn't married, I wasn't dating steady, and I was thinking, 'Where's all the guys?' I don't know, maybe the girls relate to me."

The rousing, anthematic "Sing Your Praise to the Lord" had been quite well received, but even people who didn't particularly care for Amy's rock- and pop-flavored gospel sounds loved "El Shaddai." It emerged as the clear winner, not only as the most loved tune on "Age to Age," but on any gospel album that year.

Settled into married life at last, Amy and Gary joined musical forces, with Chapman pushing aside his own career aspirations to get behind her steamrolling momentum as leader of her tour band. In effect, he abandoned his own recording and touring to be part of her projects. His solo portion of the "Age to Age" tour was a generous midsection, during which Amy exited the stage to change clothing. Talking playfully to the audience between songs, Chapman's solo was warm and witty. It was indicative of the musical direction in which Amy would continue to grow— strong original pop and rock arrangements with a mix of praise lyrics and more ambivalent, danceable, positive message songs.

Her second concert album had included the ambivalent lyrics of the Ronnie Milsap country-pop hit, "What a Difference You've Made in My Life." Through songs like "Finally," which he performed on the ninety-minute video concert cassette from that tour, Chapman was a strong proponent of a borderline musical genre that was neither full gospel nor secular pop. Most attempts to bridge that gap had fallen into the ravine until Amy hit the scene, so the route they were to take had many risks and its potential had yet to be realized. Amy was aware of the risks, but the lyrical direction was a choice she agreed with.

"Historically, anytime a gospel artist has tried to cross over, it has been just death for them in the Christian music realm," Amy reflects. "I don't understand it. I don't understand the mentality that says you can't express several sides of your life. B. J. Thomas does it but he's highly criticized, and unfairly so. A person is a person and you have feelings. You know, I love my husband, I struggle in my relationship with my family, this is what I feel like when I'm driving home from work, this is how I brush my teeth. Not everything has some heavy spiritual emphasis. But I feel like there have been so few gospel artists that there's a real protective feeling in the gospel music industry."

From the time Chapman became Amy's husband and bandleader, his lyrical influence would become as important to the following developments in Amy's music as Brown Bannister's production quality and directions were. His influence would guide her along the career path that Blanton and Harrell were meticulously mapping out for her and for themselves.

As early as 1981, Dan Harrell was telling *Billboard* magazine reporter Ed Morris that the Christian artists that Blanton/Harrell Productions managed were being groomed to meet the secular entertainment world on its own terms. Harrell saw a family and young teen market developing as a positive alternative to rock 'n' roll's perceived excesses.

Amy continued to soft peddle the idea that she might have pop aspirations. She was, frankly, oblivious to the business side and put all her energies into each new performance or recording session. The Blanton and Harrell roster receiving their unique guidance included Amy, Gary, Brown Bannister, Pam Mark Hall, Kathy Troccoli, Christian comedy quartet Ariel, Billy Sprague, and Jim Webber. Harrell said of his company's services to their acts, "We teach them how to walk, talk, eat, and dress. And we provide a range of accounting and investing services—if they're making money."

The innovative, full-service production company also kept its eggs solely in the contemporary Christian basket. "We wouldn't handle a Southern gospel act unless we had a Divine revelation," Harrell told *Billboard.* "Musically, we're just not there."

Musically they were on top as the new year rolled around. "Age to Age" had become the talk of the gospel industry. When the Gospel Music Association held its annual Dove Awards Show in Nashville in 1983, it was truly Amy's night. There were six Dove Awards given that night which related to the success of "Age to Age." Amy swept the field, taking honors for Best Gospel Performance in the contemporary category for the album and receiving the top honor as Gospel Artist of the Year. Michael Card and John Thompson carried home Dove Award trophies for "El Shaddai" as Gospel Song of the Year, while Card was named Songwriter of the Year.

Even the packaging was judged by the GMA membership to be superlative. Designer Dennis Hill and photographer Michael Borum received Doves for the Gospel Record Album Cover of the Year for their work on "Age to Age." The only nomination that did not result in a win for Amy that night was the Female Vocalist of the Year, which prophetically went to Sandi Patti.

Sandi Patti's win indicated something that would continue to be true of the gospel industry, which does not in general embrace Amy. It does not take well to secular-style hype. Television specials, sexy album covers, splashy and, to traditionalists, sometimes embarrassing press coverage arranged by a high-powered West Coast publicity agency and A&M Records is certainly out of the ordinary for a gospel act. The gospel establishment recognizes Amy for her accomplishments, but they suspect her success is more attributable to the pop-rock music than to the religious content of her lyrics, especially in light of the decline in that content in recent years. Some even wonder if the Amy Grant team has not simply been using gospel as a convenient launchpad for their pop thrust all along.

There can be no denying that megasuccess in any field

breeds jealousy. There are probably many gospel acts, especially in her category, who would give their eyeteeth for half the media exposure that Amy has garnered. Success and pop aspirations certainly contribute to Amy's status as an outsider within the kingdom she would seem to dominate. Amy's inability to repeat her 1983 sweeps in the Dove Awards is in part attributable to the fact that there are other acts in her category of Inspirational or contemporary Christian female vocalists, notably Sandi Patti, whose solidly rib-rocked gospel and hymnal emphases leave no doubt in the mainstream gospel community where their allegiances lie.

Yet, the 1983 Dove Awards bounty gave Amy a big boost. The media attention she garnered as a result of that GMA Awards sweep multiplied when she carried off a 1983 Grammy Award, secular music's greatest accolade, in NARAS's gospel category as well. A quick spate of press stories made it appear that Amy Grant had suddenly burst from out of nowhere. To the secular press, she practically had.

The extra exposure generated by her sweep of the 1983 GMA Dove Award ceremonies boosted ticket sales at her concerts and record sales to new levels. Blanton and Harrell had taken another step that further distanced them from traditional gospel music in the way they conducted Amy's concert business. Instead of utilizing the promoters who had booked her early tour dates, they went outside those circles to contract for regional tour packages with a handful of major promoters who had little experience with gospel, but wide experience with general family entertainment and rock concerts. Harrell still saw benefit in keeping her performance dates down to eighty or eighty-five shows a year, rather than filling all the requests that came in.

"We don't tour as much as a lot of people do," Harrell explains. "Eventually, it will take away from an artist's creativity."

Mike Blanton and Dan Harrell moved through a select list of promoters to medium-sized concert halls where secular stars also played. While newspaper articles told and retold the story of Amy's fast approach to a gold record through the autumn of 1983, Blanton and Bannister picked tunes for her next big album.

Amy and Gary would take a trip to Colorado's famed Caribou Ranch recording center with as many members of their family as could get away. It became a combination family reunion and recording session for "A Christmas Album." This holiday record was released with the single "Tennessee Christmas" in time for the holiday season in 1983, but the next big career move would be the album "Straight Ahead." "Tennessee Christmas" was one of Blanton and Harrell's first secular-market probes with Amy's music. It got enough air play to make the country charts, which brought a surprise nomination as a Best New Female Vocalist finalist in the Academy of Country Music's Hat Awards in 1984. Though it was finally certified as a gold record in early 1986, it didn't generate enough initial sales action to justify pointing Amy's music toward that market. Her appeal was broad enough to target the same young family and teen market that went to concerts by top country acts, but most of her newer music was pop-sounding.

"Probably one of the biggest frustrations in the contemporary Christian field is the exposure problem," explains Mike Blanton. "The question is what is the best avenue to go down in order to reach more people."

In December of that year, Amy got her biggest Christmas present a few weeks early. The Recording Industry Association of America (RIAA) certified that "Age to Age" had sold more than five hundred thousand copies, and it presented her with their coveted Gold Record plaque. Sales by gospel-only acts were not previously so closely documented. Shut off from most opportunities for in-store

There was a meeting of gospel music giants as Gary and Amy got together backstage at the Gospel Music Association Dove Awards show to chat with Pat Boone and GMA executive director Don Butler.　　Photo courtesy of Gospel Music Association

Amy and Gary live here in this old Southern colonial mansion surrounded by the pastures of Riverstone Farm.

Photo by Bob Millard

These ladies could be gospel music's "Million Dollar All-Girls Quartet." Seen here (l–r) are Kelly Nelon Thompson (Rex Nelon Singers), Sherri Williamson (Lewis Family), Tanya Goodman (Happy Goodman Family), and Amy Grant.   Photo by Alan Mayor

The Dove Awards added up in 1983 when Amy was responsible for wins in six different categories. Beaming in the background is a proud producer, the bearded Brown Bannister.

Photo by John McCormick

Amy signs an autograph for a fan. Photo by Alan Mayor

A moving moment in Amy Grant's concert. Photo by Alan Mayor

The reigning princess of pop-gospel looks forward to going
home after a long concert tour.   Photo by Chip Mitchell

Family and friends surround Amy to congratulate her on receiving this platinum record commemorating sales of one million copies of "Age to Age." Among well-wishers pictured here are manager/brother-in-law Dan Harrell (third from left), husband Gary Chapman, and comanager Mike Blanton (far right).

Photo by Jeffrey Mayer

sales, gospel acts had sold records from concert stages and from the tour bus after shows. Those sales did not fall under the RIAA survey toward gold-record status.

Amy's management claimed for her the title of first solo gospel artist to win a gold album. Although she was the first solo artist in the contemporary Christian music category to earn such an honor, there were other solo acts before her who earned gold records for gospel music. Tennessee Ernie Ford, whose career has spanned country music hits and television acting, had most of his recognition in the recording arts as a gospel artist, earning the first RIAA gold album for gospel in 1955 for his Capitol Records album "Hymns."

In 1958 a young fellow named Laurie London scored a major hit record with the Sunday School sing-along "He's Got the Whole World in His Hands" and earned a gold single citation. Ernie Ford's 1961 album "Spirituals" went gold, as did his 1962 release "Nearer the Cross." The gospel credentials of the Mormon Tabernacle Choir can hardly be assailed, and their album, "The Lord's Prayer," went gold in 1963. That same year a French Catholic religious sister named Soeur Sourire undoubtably became the first woman of pure gospel credentials to sell 500,000 records for a gold album with her record "The Singing Nun." It is interesting to note that for all the comparisons between Elvis Presley and Amy Grant, after her initial breakthrough, Presley actually earned two gold albums for gospel recordings, "How Great Thou Art" (1968) and "His Hand in Mine" (1969), before Amy had picked up her first guitar. For all Presley's accomplishments, history will note that the only Grammy Award accorded him came with that first gospel effort.

None of this detracts from the new life that Amy's commercial success injected into the gospel community, nor from the public attention she helped focus on gospel artists and their music. The two other contemporary Christian albums to earn gold record status before hers, "The Music Machine" (Sparrow) and a choral work called "Allelujia" (Benson Company), had failed to capture the general public's imagination the way this fresh-faced Nashville girl's work did.

Since that time such solo acts as Dallas Holm and Sandi Patti have equaled that mark, as have Amy's later albums. Amy broke that barrier for the first time, whipping up a whirlwind of national media attention. The message that got through to her fans was that she really cared about them, more than she cared about selling records, concert tickets, tour books, and T-shirts. Her attitude contributed to the selling of more records, concert tickets, tour books, and T-shirts than ever before.

"There's even more of an intensity about this for myself because I know how long I can do this and I don't want it to interfere with my family," Amy explained at the time she collected the first gold record. "I'm twenty-three right now, but my prime target audience when I am singing is high school and college age. I'm trying to tell them something that I think is going to be important in their life. I want to be helping them to make a decision about their life.

"For me to relate to them and them say, 'She's got something to say,' I don't know if I can still do that when I'm forty. So there's this feeling that I've got to do it now, before I'm too old, or they'll listen to me like they listen to their mom."

Bringing the message of their faith and Christian-based life-style to more people and selling more copies of Amy's records were complementary aims for the management team. Songs chosen for "Straight Ahead" and the increasingly polished stage presentation and props all pointed to a crossover direction—pop music. The album cover art borrowed wholesome blue-jeaned sex appeal from the Brooke Shields school of modeling. None of the tunes from "Straight Ahead" were played on regular rock and adult contemporary radio on a steady basis, but it wasn't from lack of trying. Word, Inc. commissioned an MTV-style music video for a tune called "It's Not a Song." Amy penned the tune herself, her first nongospel or Christian life-style recording. It was a bit premature in that it found few secular television outlets, but then Blanton and Harrell have consistently led the pack in creating trends rather than following them.

Among Amy's growing résumé of television appearances at that time was a syndicated 1983 Multimedia Entertainment Christmas special, "The Gift of Song," produced by Nashville's Scene Three Productions. She was also tapped for Dick Clark's "Salute to Lou Rawls." She was able to choose what she would sing, a Russ Taff song instead of the old standby gospel tunes the show's director originally asked her to sing. The spring of 1984 saw Amy make her debut as a television actress in "Story Songs and Stars," another Multimedia/Scene Three project which the 7-Up Company underwrote. Amy played a mousy secretary who dreamed of becoming a professional singer. Her part was the female lead, opposite songwriter/singer/actor Paul Williams.

"I will be singing his praises for a long time," Amy says of her diminutive costar. "He was so confident and secure of his talent. He spent a lot of time helping others in the show."

The "It's Not a Song" video became part of that television special, for which Amy claims, in typical self-deprecating humor, she was best qualified to play her part because she was still a complete stranger to the nongospel world.

"One of the characters was to be an unknown who could sing and, as far as television audiences go, I'm lower than unknown," she says.

The awards and media exposure were beginning to pile up. While Amy was filming her part for the television special, Gary was working up arrangements with Michael W.

Smith for Amy's biggest stage show to that time, The Straight Ahead Tour. Special lighting, stage props, commemorative jewelry, and traffic-light pendants to match the Straight Ahead visual theme were being readied.

By the time Amy and Gary were ready to open the extended 1984 Straight Ahead Tour on home turf in February, in Jackson Hall at the Tennessee Performing Arts Center, it was getting harder and harder to make the statement that Amy could be "lower than unknown."

Chapter 11

"Age to Age" stayed at the top of the gospel-record charts for twenty-two consecutive months. In 1984 it was bumped from the top position by her own followup, "Straight Ahead," which came out that spring. "Age to Age" continued to enjoy sales so solid that an unheard of one million copies was being bandied about as that record's likely plateau. Amy would earn gospel's first platinum record and raise her stock in the general entertainment business to the level of successful pop and rock acts. Her growing status as a record seller and a hometown heroine got her an invitation to Nashville's favorite annual rock 'n' roll party—Charlie Daniels' Volunteer Jam. Ten thousand paying "guests" and about three thousand backstage invitees packed the arena and lower deck of the city's Municipal Auditorium in 1984. As always, the Jam featured a musical montage of top country, rock, jazz, and sometimes gospel talent, ending in a free-for-all jam that lasted from about midnight until Charlie Daniels called it off. The Vol Jam was recorded by the cameras of a Dick Clark television crew taping for a musical special.

That first Volunteer Jam appearance came during Amy's winter at-home period. She and Gary were able to take a bit of rest from their touring and recording schedules to give

their private lives some thought. Settled in a sparsely deco-
rated, multistory condo in fashionable Belle Meade, Amy
and Gary realized that her career was already too big to
allow them to start the family she wanted. Nor would Amy
soon return to Vanderbilt to take the twenty credits she
needed to graduate.

"The only thing I can think of right now is that I probably
should finish school before Gary and I start a family," Amy
explained.

Gary had made arrangements for the "Straight Ahead"
album preview tour, working up songs to test in front of
audiences before they were laid down on tape at Caribou
Ranch studio. Amy accepted that, much as she desired to
have children of her own, she would have to make do for
the time being with her role as Aunt Amy to her sisters'
offspring.

"I don't think it's physically possible to be a mother and
do what I'm doing now," Amy said. "We'll probably wait a
lot longer than most of our friends who got married at the
same time. We might have one child who's real adaptable to
the road and a second child who can't sleep unless he's in
his baby bed.

"I used to think how great it would be to have four kids; a
mama with ducklings. They're not objects. My sister says
everyone [who has a child] chooses to have a child. You
have a commitment to become totally involved in every
need they have. They're persons, not objects or posses-
sions. I have seven nieces and nephews, the oldest one is
six. And seven fall within three and a half years of each
other. You can take any group and see how they react. For a
nephew, just being there is enough. For a niece, she has to
have your undivided attention. That is the unplanned vari-
able with kids."

Amy and Gary put a lot of care and planning into the
Straight Ahead Tour. It was launched with the most exciting stage set and lighting and possibly the loudest sound

system in gospel music. It sold out at one major rock hall after another coast-to-coast. The West Coast secular music business paid little heed to the wholesomely sexy young gospel singer from Nashville when she was booked at their prestigious Universal Amphitheatre in Hollywood—until she sold out the first night almost as quickly as advance tickets could be exchanged for money. A second performance was scheduled and it also sold out.

Amy and Gary spent extra time in Los Angeles in December of 1983, trying, in Chapman's words, "to get more exposure." As the sun went down over the smoggy Hollywood hills, Amy and Gary sat gazing from the balcony of their hotel room. The shadow of a skyscraper moved inexorably across the deep blue water of the hotel pool, still swimmable in California's temperate Christmas season. For Amy, more accustomed to the eagerness of Nashville syndicators to get her before a television camera, the L.A. trip was grueling. But she made at least one contact that would lead to all-important network television exposure.

"I felt like meat on a hook," Amy told *Contemporary Christian Music* magazine. "We'd go to places like Johnny Carson. The talent director would take me into the inner sanctum while Gary and my manager sat outside taking bets on how I'd do."

Other major entertainment capitals were also slow to recognize her increasing success. In April of 1984 the New York *Times* took note of her in an article headlined, "Amy Grant: On Top But Unknown." As she was in the midst of a three-month tour that did not include a Manhattan concert date, the newspaper remarked upon her success-without-fame thusly: ". . . what are we to make of a popular singer who has won every award in her field, including a Grammy; topped the charts for months on end; tours constantly; is played all the time on the radio; and seems not only to be unknown in New York, but unknowable?" When she sold out two concerts at Radio City Music Hall later that year, the *Times* got its answer. Amy's popularity had spread even into the heart of the Big Apple.

Amy was rapidly turning lyrics with religious and secular meanings and pop and rock melodies into mainstream potential. Despite fundamentalist disapproval and gospel industry jealousy, she was certainly the most salable religious artist of the modern day. As ever bigger sales potential loomed over the gospel music industry, questions of the conflicts between profit margins and ministry cropped up with ever increasing urgency in some quarters. Ambivalent lyrics were where the big dollars were but was it where the ministry of Christ belonged? As GMA's Don Butler put it: "There is no such thing as gospel 'music'—the lyrics are what make songs religious or secular."

There had previously been little movement toward pop by gospel acts trying to keep their Christian emphasis. Substantial traffic had come the other way starting in the late seventies, but Amy was poised to break the barriers against pop acceptance of more than the occasional religious tune like George Harrison's "My Sweet Lord" or the oft-recorded "People Get Ready." In the late sixties the Northern California State Youth Choir changed its name to the Edwin Hawkins Singers and had a big hit with a rollicking version of a two-hundred-year-old hymn called "Oh Happy Day," but Amy's songs seemed to score with a wider audience primarily because the words were not hymn-heavy in any way. A huge inner-industry debate concerning cash-flow emphasis versus ministry became part of the GMA's Gospel Music Week seminar sessions in 1983 and 1984.

The argument of whether rock music is morally adaptable to Christian lyrics was an old one. Paul Baker authored a book called *Why Should the Devil Have All the Good Music* in 1979 to answer critics of contemporary rock 'n' gospel sounds. The argument, as such, was never settled, though market acceptance of contemporary Christian artists has mooted the point. Acceptance of more scripturally oriented talents such as Sandi Patti, Michael Card, Michael W. Smith, and the 1985 return of Cynthia Clawson to recording and touring have made just as much impact on the growth of Christian entertainment as such glittering, smoke bomb-using gospel rock acts as Stryper and Petra.

Amy's careerings toward a place in the secular music business for her ever lighter praise and Christian life-style music made her a standout even among gospel-rockers. Rumors flew that Amy was about to become a pop singer instead of a contemporary Christian artist. Some of the criticism that came her way was seen in her camp as jealousy. Amy told one newspaper reporter after another that she didn't want to become a pop star, while Dan Harrell continued making statements like, "If Lionel [Richie] called—we'd do it in a minute."

Amy's denials of the obvious next step in her career were more truth than deception in her own mind. Indeed, Amy didn't want to be a star at all, but she did want a wider audience for her music.

"I want to reach out to new people," Amy explains. "But not at the risk of the songs . . . I'm not a rock 'n' roll monster, but it's exciting with the staging, the lights, good sound and stuff."

The move had been planned by Blanton and Harrell for a couple of years. It would be implemented in high gear once they decided on A&M to distribute Word's Myrrh Records product through secular outlets. Amy was about to do what many others in the gospel music industry probably wished they could do, but were either too closely tied to the fundamentalists and church organizations to risk or too evangelistic to be successful. No one in Amy Grant's camp cared if the traditionalists and old guard castigated her music: They were aiming at a younger, more upscale audience of Christian youth.

"Parents encourage their kids to go see Amy because her lyrics are clean, they're acceptable, and her venues are wholesome," explains GMA executive director Don Butler. "She doesn't want the conservative fundamentalists coming to her concerts. She wants young people who will get up and move to the beat, people who want to be pinned against the back wall by the volume for two hours. That's what she gives them. Besides, Amy never had the traditional gospel music fans, so how could she turn them off? She has never been the darling of the fundamentalists."

At the fifteenth annual Dove Awards ceremonies, in 1984, Amy was largely bested by a stout, blond mother-to-be about her own age—Sandi Patti. Sandi sang to a traditional church audience and benefited as much from the backlash against Amy's pop directions as from her own considerable talents. Sandi Patti took Doves as Female Vocalist of the Year, Album of the Year—Inspirational, Artist of the Year. Additionally, the title tune to her album "More Than Wonderful" brought Gospel Song of the Year honors for writer Lanny Wolfe and left to the Amy Grant crowd only Gospel Music Album Cover of the Year honors for the people who created the cover art for "A Christmas Album." Amy was stung by criticism that she was deserting the fold, but she was getting used to fundamentalists criticizing every move she made, including her television-special appearances.

"I got some negative feedback because of my special," Amy says. "In my own life I find I criticize things I'm frightened of. I think the root of the criticism is that some people don't know my motives."

She had always been honest about her music. She had never intended to be solely a hymn and scripturally oriented praise singer like Sandi Patti in the first place.

"I don't feel like I'm a preacher," Amy says. "And I don't have the wisdom to be a great teacher, but I'm honest."

Her songs and statements, rife as they sometimes are with the breezy imprecision of preppy slang, reach her audience on an emotional level. Fan attachment defies critics who point out differences between the mainstream church's gospel message and music and Amy's positive, but often light, encouragement of Christian faith and life-style through her art.

"There are a lot of songs that I just write and the only differentiation between them and secular pop music that I would say is that they are an observation of everyday life from a Christian perspective," Amy explains. "Like, I wrote a great song about my great grandmother one time and somebody who was really serious about what the lyrics should say might say, 'You know, you say you're a Christian singer, but I've played this song about your great grandmother for my friend and they were not saved. You're a failure.' A hard-line gospel songwriter might say that. But my point of view would be that instead of just writing about this one little piece of the spectrum, I'm just, as a songwriter, approaching life."

Bolstered by her teamwork relationship with her husband and a growing sense of security in her art, Amy quickly got over her disappointment at the turnabout of fortunes between the 1983 and 1984 Dove Awards ceremonies.

"[In 1983] I felt like Miss Piggy," Amy told Nashville television interviewer Dan Miller. "In fact I called myself Miss Piggy because every time I turned around I was getting an award, to the point of getting a little embarrassed. Then the next year I felt like we worked so much harder. We'd just been on the road, I'd done tons, we'd sold a lot of albums, and we didn't get anything. So the Dove Awards, it's really funny, it's family. We all do the same thing. So sometimes the whole camaraderie system will choose to honor one person and sometimes it's somebody else."

If she did poorly at the Dove Awards that year, the Grammy's were better to her than she expected. In the early eighties, the gospel music business differed substantially from other industries in that singles, while mailed to radio stations for play, were not available in the marketplace. Gospel fans wanted entire albums by their favorites, not just one song. Gospel radio was not geared for the "hits" mentality of pop stations, either. Gospel deejays were winning souls—not ratings points.

Word Records took a page from the disco music book of promotional gambits, floating a special medley of Amy Grant tunes on a seven-inch 33⅓ rpm disc as a promotional tool to sell more copies of "Age to Age." Of course, by late fall 1985, excess copies of "Age to Age" were offered on television as free premiums with a $14.95 three-record compilation of contemporary Christian artists. Named "Sing Your Praise to the Lord" after one of Amy's hits, it featured top Inspirational and contemporary youth acts including Michael W. Smith. But, the odd-sized "Ageless Medley" single caught on and brought Amy her second Grammy as Best Gospel Performance—Female. The win was so unexpected that Blanton/Harrell Productions had Amy playing a concert in Memphis instead of sitting with the celebrities in Los Angeles the night the awards were announced.

As the album followed the test run of a preview tour, "Straight Ahead" rolled on through 1984 as a dramatic step forward for Amy's recording and showmanship. On stage, she had not turned away from witnessing her faith, but eight years of experience had made her more powerful as a performer. The stage sets and lighting dazzled the eye as on no previous Amy Grant tour. The traffic-light motif that dominated the backdrop featured only green light arrows pointing heavenward. Near the end of a well-paced and -choreographed show, a truly stunning visual effect complemented the rising crescendo of the song "Straight Ahead." The dramatic graphics seen at the Nashville premier of the show were programmed to raise hair on the backs of necks wherever the show played.

Indeed, it did. A student reviewer for the University of

Mississippi campus newspaper, obviously new to the Charismatic experience about which Amy was singing, described the effect of the dramatic finale: "Then something really neat happened. Gold stars formed along the sides of the 'highway' and the road even seemed to me to expand. Then the words 'Straight Ahead' cut across the top half of the highway—bingo, a gold cross. As I sat looking at the cross and the concert came to an end, I wondered about a lot of things I had seen and heard that night."

Though the early steps taken by Amy's management to find an opening in either country or pop-record and video-broadcast outlets had met with only limited interest, there were signs that success was soon to be within their grasp. Where Amy had been lucky to get booked on a Billy Graham revival and a string of dates opening for the Bill Gaither Trio a few years earlier, she was hot enough by the summer of 1984 to open concerts for top country-pop crooner, Kenny Rogers. As the gates to the big-time pop music world swung open before her, Amy knew that she would not compromise her art or message—but she was terrified with pure stage fright.

"It's one thing to sing in front of people who paid to see Amy Grant," she explained about her Kenny Rogers opening stand. "I mean, at one of my concerts I can see the kids singing along with me, just like I do at a James Taylor concert."

Scared stiff before one of the early nights of that tour as Rogers's warmup act, waiting in the wings for her call to the stage, Amy was reassured when a couple of young fans approached her with a message of support.

"One girl threw her arms around me and said, 'I'm so glad you're here, your music has changed my life,'" Amy reveals. "This huge lump nestled in my throat. I felt like you do when your dad comes to your first basketball game."

Kenny Rogers enjoyed Amy and the band so much that

he offered to record a duet with her. Rogers is almost guaranteed a Top Five record—if not a Number One— anytime he releases even a half decent song. After hearing that the song he had in mind had been turned down by no less a vocalist than Aretha Franklin because the range required was too great for her voice, Amy knew she had better pass on the opportunity too. When she was overwhelmed by the powerful scat singing of Patti LaBelle on the latter's 1985 Thanksgiving television special, she would undoubtedly be reminded that she had to be careful who she sang with. Amy makes no bones about being a stylist rather than a powerful vocalist. But, at that time, she recorded a duet with gospel-rocker Randy Stonehill.

The attention of the secular music world was drawn to Amy at every turn that year. Offers to sign up with a couple of labels were submitted to Blanton and Harrell, who gave them serious scrutiny. Such a deal would have to come on their terms, as had just about every other significant development in Amy's career to that time.

"I'm not thinking if I could get a duet with Willie Nelson I'd have it made," Amy explained, as early negotiations began in secret between Word Records, Blanton and Harrell, and A&M Records for a distribution deal. The deal reportedly gave A&M options to distribute Amy Grant and the rest of Word Records's catalog in secular outlets. Word's sublabels by that time included the Blanton/Harrell label Reunion Records, created in the mid-1980s to include most of the acts they managed.

Amy was on the verge of having the pop market expertise and muscle of a major secular label behind her, yet, true to her approach to her whole career, she was not hungry for it. Writing and performing with Gary Chapman and close friends like Michael W. Smith, Brown Bannister, and Kathy Troccoli had finally brought her to a level of security about herself and her music, so she no longer felt compelled to defend herself or her art from either gospel or secular critics. If she got a shot at secular air play and distribution, that would be great, if not, she would be happy then, too. It was, perhaps, this last step in the maturation of the reticent contemporary Christian superstar that prepared her for the tough world outside the protective Christian community.

"There is a point at which we all have to say we're satisfied," she says. "I can't let the number of albums I sell dictate what I think of myself. If you start equating a song with dollar signs, you'll lose your value of what a song is all about."

From the release of "Age to Age" on, life became increasingly demanding for Amy and Gary, with little time for them to get away from music. When they did isolate some time, they always seemed to gravitate back into the loving circle of the Grant family in Nashville. Sometimes, though, Amy just wanted to flee the mounting pressures of her growing stardom. She has often made statements about disliking the offstage by-products of being a star.

"Sometimes everything just seems so hectic I just want to fly away to Switzerland and not tell anyone where I am," she complains. "Starting over in a little village where nobody could care less who I am, much less understand me— to just start over from scratch, to be responsible for my actions, not just the upkeep of my reputation."

When the A&M/Word deal was cut, little notice was taken outside the music trade. Amy had barnstormed the print and broadcast media through 1983 and 1984, appearing in the pages of *Life, Time, Grit, USA Today,* on ABC-TV's "Good Morning America," "Merv Griffin," "Entertainment Tonight," and on syndicated television specials. It has long been one of Amy Grant's greatest personal gifts that she appeals to reporters almost as much as she does to her young fans.

Reporters covering entertainment beats are not used to talking to artists who open up so immediately on such personal levels as Amy. Amy is a compelling, big-eyed beauty whose unguarded replies to questions make her eminently quotable. Amy has consistently gotten good press because she *is* good press. Most gospel artists have carefully crafted replies, genuine or not, that make interviews sound almost like gospel award acceptance speeches or the call and response platitudes of a tent revival. Wholly without pretense, committed to what she believes, Amy expresses herself with an outspoken flamboyance that she sometimes regrets later, but which usually makes what newspaper men call "great copy." She rarely puts her most sanctimonious foot forward.

Back in Nashville, it was time to settle in with her creative clique of close friends and begin putting together a musical package, album, and stage show to do what had never been done—to go "pop" without losing her essential Christian base. Working with her husband, who had his finger on the pulse of both musical worlds even much earlier, helped Amy face her greatest career challenge.

"I've had couples come up and say, 'Boy, we'd kill each other if we worked together that much,' " Amy says. "But Gary and I met in a working relationship. We're used to rubbing shoulders and bumping heads. I think it would be kind of lonely out there knowing that your husband was back home."

Insiders say that the songwriting collaboration between Amy and Gary largely consists of Amy getting something started and Gary applying his skills as "the song doctor" to finish it off. Yet both feel that their collaborative work on "Straight Ahead" and "Unguarded" is the most cohesive of their careers.

"[It's] a real team effort between us, the band, and everyone else involved," Amy says.

Gary's input in her music became apparent within a year of their marriage, when his name appeared with Mike Blanton and Dan Harrell's as executive producer of "Straight Ahead," then again for the album "Unguarded." Amy and

Gary work closely together as a husband/wife team, with Gary contributing greatly to her musical direction and overseeing the details of her live show.

"I get a lot of enjoyment out of what I do," says Chapman, who virtually gave up his own solo career to integrate his efforts with Amy's. "I guess it could seem like a problem. You know, she brings home the bacon and I eat it, but I've gotten so involved in what she's doing that it's really a team effort and totally fulfilling."

"Gary's really great," she said. "Sensitive—maybe too much so—but that's balanced by a terrific sense of humor. Like most couples, we fight about everything. 'You're so pushy,' he'll say. 'Stop manipulating me,' I'll say. It's a great marriage."

To raise general public awareness of Amy's impending bid for pop-radio acceptance, Amy gave interviews to *Time* magazine and the Bible of rock music, *Rolling Stone* magazine. By some quirk of publishers' timetables, both appeared the same week in the spring of 1985. The *Time* piece was shared with other contemporary Christian acts, but the glare of *Rolling Stone*'s hip secular-music journalism illuminated Amy directly for the rock world. Examined seriously for the first time by no-holds-barred rock writers, Amy and Gary's at-home edge and opinions seemed a little more hip and flip than a lot of her more conservative fans were ready to accept. Amy talked about skinny-dipping on a deserted beach in South Africa, rock star Prince and his simulated masturbation, and (possibly the gravest admission as far as some gospel fans were concerned) that she intended to be a pop artist. The article was a success in that it got the desired exposure for Amy in the secular music community, but there was an emotional price to pay for her honesty. Her feelings were hurt by adverse reaction from conservative fans, though her overall career was unscathed.

Contemporary Christian Music magazine chronicled the letter-writing backlash, offering space for the Blanton and

Harrell apologia. There was no retraction of Amy's statements, however. "That's the way she is. She's very frank," said a Word Records spokesman in her defense. GMA's Don Butler, a longtime observer of his industry, noted that the backlash against Amy was not debilitating, in contrast to B. J. Thomas's experience. Thomas lost money and fans, got booed and spat upon, while Amy suffered no financial setbacks from the limited fan disapproval. The sale of her $20 sweatshirts never missed a lick at concert concession stands.

In Detroit, Amy was confronted by young fans who presented her with a bouquet of flowers attached to a note that read: "Turn back. You can still be saved if you renounce what you've done."

"I cried in the shower, then went into the room and Gary was in bed, and I said, 'Would you hold me for a while?' and I just cried," Amy confesses. "Gary prayed for us, then the words of my pastor echoed in my head: "You are called to love them."

Pastor Don Finto may have expressed those words of comfort backstage before one of the nightly prayer circles Amy and her crew and band always form before a show. At the request of Amy and Gary, Finto periodically accompanies them on the road for a few days to counsel and pray with them during the long periods when they have to be away from Belmont Church.

"I spend two nights," Pastor Finto explains. "One night I'll ride on the bus with them to the next place, then another night and I'll come on home. I'm just there, I'm just available to talk with them. I try to find out where they are. I probe where I get the opportunity. I challenge, we worship, we pray. I don't do it for this purpose, but naturally I have input. Anywhere I am I have input. Many times I will make notes on places where I think they can get the message across clearer."

Through the *Rolling Stone* episode, Amy was coming to

understand that she would be held responsible for anything she blurted out to a reporter. Secular writers would not automatically edit out statements that might reflect badly on her as the Christian music press and local papers always had.

"The interview I did with *Rolling Stone* upset some people," Amy says. "When I read it, I was a little embarrassed. Sometimes in conversation you say things that don't translate well into print. The media attention has been refreshing, but sometimes I screw up."

The flurry of complaints about Amy's new musical tone and the *Rolling Stone* interview that summer was all just so much wind that would blow over. Concerts in 6,000- to 12,000-seat halls continued to sell out across the country for the Unguarded Tour. Now that her music had reached the pop and adult contemporary "easy listening" charts, Amy-mania was unstoppable.

Chapter 12

As 1985 dawned, everybody in the Grant family and Blanton and Harrell circles knew the moment they'd been working toward for the past several years had finally come. Amy gained tremendous national attention in February 1985 when she sang "Angels" on the Grammy Awards show. Her music was broadcast worldwide when she made her second appearance at Charlie Daniels's Volunteer Jam earlier that month. A satellite linkup not only made Daniels's eleventh annual Nashville homecoming concert the longest pay-per-view subscription concert in cable history, it also was carried extensively on Voice of America overseas.

When "Unguarded" finally hit secular and Christian record racks in June of 1985, it hit with all the promotional pomp and circumstance of any pop diva's product. A&M created posters, buttons, stand-up cardboard statues of Amy, and, most importantly, saturation distribution of the album itself. Perhaps to heighten the visual appeal of Amy's pop debut, Word produced four different covers, each a little different, from the same dreamy black and white photo session, and punctuated by hot-pink lettering.

Gary had help from professional show designers in putting together the Unguarded Tour stage package. Hundreds of computer-controlled lights hung above the stage and smoke generators pumped out clouds of rock 'n' roll fog at dramatic moments.

Amy had grown in her profession to the point where Blanton and Harrell felt she and her music were ready to enter the big leagues. There was no overt religiousness to the staging of the Unguarded Tour. In its place was a Lawrence Welk-style bubble-making machine and an uproarious skit featuring keyboardists in uniforms playing make-believe horns behind pink and black bandstands. New choreography had Amy and most of the band locking arms to kick in the style of Radio City Music Hall Rockettes. Amy herself hopped and kicked more than ever before throughout the program, in a series of lively choreographed steps dubbed by Nashville *Tennessean* reviewer Robert K. Oermann as "the Amy."

Gospel, as an all-inclusive category, has moved much of its record sales into stores, where RIAA tabulations now say it accounts for 7 percent of all record and tape sales—more than either classical or jazz sounds. Record buyers reportedly spent as much as $75 million on gospel records in 1984 and that figure was expected to be topped by 1985's sales. Amy's Inspirational/contemporary Christian music has become representative of the biggest-selling branch of that category, much to the dismay of the more traditional stylists and the uncountable local family trios and quartets who consider their own music the true gospel music.

"I can't speak for the old-line gospel singers, but I would imagine that it's probably—for them artistically—it's a little disconcerting for people to start associating gospel music with contemporary," Amy said sympathetically.

Amy's ascension to new heights as a contemporary Christian singer with an increasing exposure to mainstream pop fans has brought peripheral economic opportunities. Just as top professional athletes become spokesmen for shaving products and light beer, Amy was drawn into audio and video product endorsements. In 1985 Amy regularly rocked out in clips from her Age to Age concert video to promote Curtis Mathes big-screen televisions, while Sony featured her in magazine ads for their cassettes.

Amy came to realize that eventual success, or lack of it, as a gospel singer in the pop music world will depend on two factors: pop fans' willingness to accept her on her own, admittedly less than rabid, terms as a witness to her religion; and her gospel fans' ability to accept her as a broader-based singer, "an entertainer who also happens to be a Christian." Ambivalence has been a key element in Amy's musical trek toward pop. Her image has developed intentionally without major emphasis on preaching so that Amy's music and shows can be understood according to each person's own interpretation. Amy knows what she intends to convey, but the audience must add its own interpretations to create the complete meaning. This strategy widens her potential audience considerably, as each individual listener can load as much or as little religious emphasis as he or she wants onto much of her newer music.

"I feel like in the past we have felt, we as Christian artists have felt like every song, every album had to encompass everything that means to be Christian," she says. "I feel like a lot of us now feel like 'let's approach all aspects of life from a Christian perspective.' Now it doesn't mean that suddenly every song doesn't have to be 'Blood on the Cross.' That's never not included. But it's just saying there's so many areas of life to be discussed and it's important to have somebody discuss it from a Christian perspective. How great to have a song that says, you know, it's really bad between me and my husband but I know that love perseveres."

Amy proceeded through a long and physically demanding 1985 tour schedule. It was the most demanding on her throat because of the number of shows, and she suffered her first serious vocal-chord strain, causing cancelation of several shows around Labor Day. Her first pop-side single, "Find a Way," climbed to the Top Forty in *Billboard* charts. By the end of the year, "Unguarded" was headed out of the *Billboard* pop-album Top 100 after appearing there for thirty weeks. She seemed to have tapped that magic middle ground at a time when society was reaching for musical alternatives. Extremely committed Young Life Christian fans continued to find religious significance in such staging as spotlighting that momentarily bathed Amy in stark white light, seeing it as a symbol of purity. More secular-oriented fans just enjoyed the danceable rhythms of her top-notch band, the personal communication of Amy's anecdotes and comments from stage.

Amy's enunciation is often poor from behind a microphone, occasionally obscuring her lyrics, which, after all, are the heart of a gospel song. Many of her young fans know her lyrics by heart anyway, so they found a palatable invitation to faith in her Christian witnessing in her performance. There was the added communication of her mid-concert monolog, delivered partly while Amy lay flat on her back, legs crossed and kicking into the air like the B-grade movie stereotype of a teenager on the telephone. She came as close as she ever has to delivering a full-scale Christian witness during this part of the concert.

"For maybe five or ten minutes [during concerts], I'll say who I am and what Jesus means in my life," Amy says. "I don't want to browbeat a crowd for two hours."

At the Murfreesboro, Tennessee, homecoming concert Amy performed on her only swing by her home area during the 1985 circuit, she heard more cries of "We love you, Amy" than "Praise the Lord" from the concert hall crowd, yet she feels no compromise is needed in her softened approach. She is, more than ever, still in a financial position to remain true to her own vision of her career, which is to present a happy Christian role model and musical alternative rather than an emotional revival.

"She wants both worlds and will work hard to get both worlds," says Don Butler.

"That's one reason I started writing songs, because I didn't want to impose my religion on anyone," Amy offers. "This way my audience can sit back and draw their own conclusions, and I feel a certain freedom because I've communicated what I think and the audience's interpretation of it is its own responsibility."

Amy refuses to consider her fans as Christian and non-Christian listeners, to the extent that they may have different expectations from her. She feels that in her younger fans she is dealing with malleable minds, whether they have had contact with Christian ideas before they attend her concert or not.

"Why isolate yourself?" she asks. "Your life isolates you enough. I'm isolated when I walk into a room and somebody says, 'She's a Christian' and nobody offers me a joint and all the coke [cocaine] disappears. I don't want it anyway, but it doesn't mean that we can't be friends."

Having that family base from which to make career decisions without regard to how things have traditionally been done in the gospel industry has given manager Dan Harrell greater latitude in his business. He has been creative and in iron-fisted control of business moves. In having things their own way, Amy and Blanton/Harrell Productions have created new paths for contemporary Christian artists who are following, often skirting, the old gospel music business establishment.

"She doesn't wear chiffon dresses and have a beehive hairdo and that breaks down the gospel music stereotype," confides Harrell. "She can't be churchy. The records in the past were made for people who had a Christian experience and were very involved in the church. Now we're assuming we're going to communicate with people who may not have had that experience or even been exposed to it."

Harrell has also been of the conviction that it is best to

take new avenues to reach a new plateau. Blanton and Harrell turned over responsibility for Amy's bookings in late 1984 to rock agency Frontier Booking International (FBI), the same company that books Joan Jett and the Blackhearts and other mainline rock acts. When their agent there, John Huie, left the company to set up his own H-1 agency, they transferred the account to H-1 for continued attention by someone familiar with the workings of big-dollar, major-arena touring as well as with the philosophical framework peculiar to contemporary Christian music. They have found it more effective to deal with only a handful of big-time promoters for Amy's tour dates than with the smaller, locally based network of numerous gospel promoters with whom they had worked.

"They made a lot of people unhappy," says GMA's Don Butler. "They made some regular gospel promoters in their cities very unhappy. They felt they had supported Amy in the lean years and when the fat times came . . . There was a lot of resentment, but what they did was smart business. They have drawn huge crowds and have been featured in major media outlets, with her own syndicated TV special with Paul Williams, and other places that most gospel artists can't [draw]."

To celebrate their success and to have a pastoral setting where they could unwind from the stress of long tours, Amy and Gary purchased historic Riverstone Farm and mansion south of Nashville, in 1985. They reportedly paid Nashville *Banner* newspaper publisher Irby Simpkins more than $1 million for the mansion, a second, large, one-story brick house, and acreage. Sister Mimi and Jack Verner acquired the brick house and a substantial portion of the acreage of the original farm and Jack runs cattle on it. Now nestled far from the noise of Nashville and comfortably removed from nearby Franklin, Tennessee, Amy and Gary have finally made real their dreams from their courtship drives in the hilly, idyllic middle-Tennessee countryside.

Riverstone Farm is a magnificent rolling pasture parcel, probably encompassing more land than the Burton Farm, located close to the Harpeth River. "The big house," as main residences of old plantations are known in the region, is a typical Southern colonial mansion, complete with massive white front columns. The well-grazed pasture is surrounded by tall, old shade trees. The driveway is lined with trees and is longer than three football fields. The front gate is an imposing wrought-iron construction built into the nearly quarter-mile-long, old-stone slave fence that stands about four feet high and runs the length of the road front.

Inside are great oak floors and the rather plain, functional staircase of a working plantation, rather than the antebellum elegance of more lavish mansions in middle Tennessee, such as Andrew Jackson's Hermitage. The mansion has been renovated with modern appliances and plumbing fixtures, yet it retains a great deal of the functional charm of a big-scale working farm of an earlier generation of Southern gentry.

Despite such appearances, Amy is a star almost under protest.

"If I had my druthers, I would be at home," Amy told Tulsa *Tribune* writer Ellis Widner. "It would suit me just being Mrs. Gary Chapman. I love singing and helping bring kids to the Lord. That's important. For some reason a simple little girl from Nashville has been accepted by them."

Amy and Gary were on the road a great deal in 1985, with little time to be "at home" even when they were in Nashville. Amy says that something inside her yearns to be "the perfect wife," yet she gets lost in the neighborhood grocery store.

"I've got to tell you, in the practical ways, I really fail a lot," she says. "I was thinking about that the other day. I had gone to the grocery store and, quite honestly, living so much of the time on a bus I have not learned to cook. A grocery store is a crazy place to be because I don't know where anything is. Sometimes, just four items can take me about an hour and a half to find. So, what I do is just allot myself a lot of time and get my little shopping cart and enjoy myself."

Amy is not quite the alien to a kitchen that she jokingly claims to be. She is a tad disorganized with such housework, though.

"You don't know whether it'll take fifteen minutes or an hour to clean the house," she admits. "And it's the same with cooking meals or anything. There's no way to tell how long it'll take."

When she does strike up the stove in their fabulous rural homestead, Amy's favorite at-home specialties are spaghetti and oriental dishes.

"I really enjoy making egg rolls," she says. "The only problem is, I grew up in a family of six, so I'm used to seeing the quantity of food that my mother cooks. With just two of us, we wind up eating the same thing for a week."

Their Williamson County, Tennessee, mansion retreat offers Amy the chance to take long walks across their treeless pastureland with the Chapman family dog, Reggie. There is a large concrete-floored kennel on the property and a tennis court equipped with a ring of lights for evening play. Amy and Gary have a pair of horses and four-wheel-drive bikes. One of Amy's pastimes is to curl up with a little light reading.

"Yes, I like to read," she says. "Some of the stuff I read is just stupid. You know, silly novels. Yes, I read the Bible. I do not absorb deep-thinking books. I may plow through one for the year. I guess my attention span is too short or something. I'm not a discoverer of great books. I have read C. S. Lewis because my husband came home and said, 'You have to read this.' "

Success has not changed the emphasis Amy places on maintaining close ties to her family. Amy also likes to corral her sisters at least twice a month, when possible, for a Grant girls lunch at some local restaurant. Although Amy's life is very busy, she believes her sisters' less celebrated lives have greater work loads than her own demanding career.

"I do what comes the easiest to me and people fall in the aisles," she says. "That's the difference with music. It's a talent that people will know who you are, but that doesn't mean it's a greater talent than any other. There are times when I've felt, 'What a farce,' that my sisters work so hard with their kids and get no attention. I do what comes naturally and get enough attention for all of us and forty times more. It's a humbling thing."

In addition to her luncheons with her sisters, Amy and Gary love to participate in a relatively new Grant family tradition: the progressive dinner. It was started as a Christmas tradition in 1982, after Amy had married and the Grant household was finally an empty nest. Including grandparents' homesteads, the Grant family Christmas dinner involves stops at seven different homes, as each family serves one course in a fabulous movable feast.

"Everyone sets an elegant table, even if it's just for broccoli cheese soup," says Amy. "At my place, of course, they sit on the rug and eat off trays."

In 1985—their first Christmas in their new, picturesque, colonial farmhouse outside Franklin—Amy and Gary had finished a long year's touring schedule. The aggressive Unguarded Tour had been her most demanding ever, yet scheduled seasonal activities for the couple included singing Christmas carols in recital with the Nashville Symphony Orchestra, followed by giving food baskets to the city's less fortunate.

Christmas in Tennessee is rarely snow-covered, though even the temperate climate of the Cumberland Valley typically turns nippy around December 25. The smell of cedar wreaths and the fresh scents of many kinds of evergreen trees are familiar greetings of Christmas in Nashville households. Waxy magnolia leaves and large furry seedpods, often tied with bright red-velvet ribbons, are also favorite seasonal decorations of Nashville's gracious hostesses. The Fannie Battle Day Home for children sponsors a lovely tradition of neighborhood caroling, with warmly dressed singers stopping at houses with candles burning in their windows as a sign of welcome. Amy has participated in this local charity caroling.

Even though Amy gives of herself at such times, she does not gladly accept the role of public personality that goes with being a star, especially where her family relationships are concerned.

"With Gary and me there's so much rah! rah! rah! about Gary Chapman and Amy Grant," she complains. "I feel like we have the most fun when we just paddle around like old people. There is nothing outstanding about my way of life except that I sing.

"I hope a time comes, maybe it'll be when Gary and I mostly write, when we'll have kids and our home will be just like a hangout for our friends. I've always enjoyed my home being that way at different times, as well as those of other friends."

Amy has not been able to attend Belmont Church regularly since her big year of pop breakthrough. By keeping contact with the Belmont Assembly through visits on the road by Don Finto and various elders of the church, Amy and Gary maintain contact with their religious home base. In recent years, young singers and writers calling Belmont Church their spiritual home have represented nearly half of all contemporary-category nominations in the Gospel Music Association Dove Awards, yet it is increasingly rare for Amy or Gary to personally sing in the church.

"I can hardly sing at Belmont," Amy confesses. "Every time I get up and sing there I start to cry. It's amazing how Don's teaching is having such a far-reaching effect. So much of what I say on stage comes from Don Finto."

Another influence that the kindly and sincere pastor of

Belmont Church has had on the pair is instilling in them the importance of giving time and energy to charities and outreach ministry programs. Some—like the "714" drug rehabilitation program which takes its name from verse 14 of the seventh chapter of II Chronicles—have church ties.

"Gary and Amy are both pretty spontaneous people," offers Don Finto. "Of course, their lives are pretty regimented right now, but if they want to do something for somebody they do it. Because Amy has become so well known it's hard to be that kind of person, but they're very spontaneous and very generous people. A couple of years ago when I was with them, Amy went over to a high school in Chattanooga and spent all day singing at the high school. Last year Amy went over to the Teen Challenge Center at the Women's Center here and spent the evening with the girls. So, they're interested in people."

Amy raised $15,000 for the Nashville chapter of Teen Challenge with a 1982 charity concert held at the Tennessee Performing Arts Center. In 1985 Amy and Gary took up the lead set by rock superstar Bruce Springsteen and asked for donations of canned food for Second Harvest Food Bank in some cities where they've performed. They have made more direct contributions of time, talent, and money to work on videos for the teen antidrug campaigns of "714," and they serve on the board of directors of the program. Amy showed there were no hard feelings for her "F" in piano studies when she gave a performance to benefit Vanderbilt's Blair School of Music. There she drew a humorous comparison to a more outlandish singer from brother-in-law and comanager Dan Harrell.

Harrell has a sense of humor and is always comparing Amy's stage appearance to such pop idols as Tina Turner, because of her recent costumes of stretch-pants and leopard-skin patterned jackets.

"Why *does* he say that?" Amy remarked tongue-in-cheek when Harrell made the comparison at the April 1985 Blair

School benefit, to which she wore a red brocade tunic and black pegged pants.

The Unguarded Tour pressed on into the fall of 1985, while the album itself reached the Number 35 position in *Billboard*'s Top 100 pop-album charts, showing excellent opening strength for the A&M thrust into the pop realm. Her singles showed top strength on, if not command of, the trade publication's Adult Contemporary charts, but the point was she was being played on a broad spectrum of pop, "lite rock," and gospel stations, garnering a wider exposure of her new music than any other gospel artist had consistently done before.

Amy enjoys her thrust into the pop market quite a bit. Her first performances were solos, just Amy on stage with her guitar. She now has a sound system the equal of any act in pop music, and probably bigger than any other in the gospel field. When the smoke bombs went off during the Unguarded Tour, computer-controlled magenta, blue, and green lights whirled through the fog like the UFO running lights in the movie *"Close Encounters of the Third Kind."* Amy's equipment, band, and crew filled two buses and three tractor-trailer trucks. She sang in halls holding six thousand to twelve thousand people who have paid $11 to $12.50 to see her show. There were acts doing better on the rock charts or making more money on the concert trail, but none of her gospel compatriots could match her.

Her success continued to build during summer 1985. Amy broke records for attendance on June 6 at Del Mar County Fair with 19,500 in attendance, and at Six Flags over Texas on June 22 with a 14,000-plus gate. Her audience had grown with the Charismatic and Young Life movements, but also beyond these religious groups to include young teens, college-age fans, and young marrieds up to their mid-thirties, with their own families, who enjoy danceable pop and rock music.

"When people express shock at the idea of crossover,

they're assuming that you're leaving something essential behind," Amy said to her critics in the Christian community. "I want to keep singing what I've always sung, but I see an opportunity to do both—to sing for a larger audience and to keep singing truth. And then I just go woooooo! Do it! Go for it!"

Amy had already earned a secular-label alignment in her bid to "go for it": at the October 1984 Radio City Music Hall concerts in New York City. In the audience was Gil Friesen, president of A&M Records. He was wary of gospel music's potential to appeal to his secular record buyers, but in Amy he saw something bigger than the category.

"After the show I was a fan," Friesen admitted. "She's that good. Christian or non-Christian, she has a rapport with the audience. She's a hit artist. She's a star. What she sings and does transcends the category."

"What I want to do is to, in the way that I communicate and express myself, is to say what it means to be a vibrant Christian woman in the eighties," Amy explained. "And it doesn't mean, hey, my breasts are going to hang out over my shirt. I mean, that's gross to me. But it means to be wholesome and alive. I think a lot of times to me something that's very sexy, if you want to call it that, appealing to me is something that's very alive."

She stopped saying "maybe" to the possibility of crossing over into the country or pop industry and in 1985 announced, "I want to play hardball in this business."

"I want to be the U.S.A.'s top pop singer with the wholesome image," she says. "It's fun to fantasize with a Madonna. All through history there have been singers that projected a popular image, Carole King, Karen Carpenter. There's no balance to what kind of image is being presented to kids today. I want to be there.

"I see myself as sort of a combination performer and evangelist," Amy explains. "I hope people enjoy my singing, but at the same time I hope their lives are affected by the words."

With Blanton/Harrell Productions running the business end of her career and husband Gary Chapman in charge of the tours and much of the musical direction along with Brown Bannister, Amy is surrounded by a close-knit, family of friends and relatives who have grown in their professions step-by-step with Amy. That continuity gives her the support and balance she needs to keep focused primarily on her own life and performance. She understands and appreciates the sacrifice her husband made when he gave up his own career to contribute all his energy to hers.

"Gary is very supportive," she says. "It isn't easy for any spouse when the other is in the public eye. He told me if he had my recognition, that was what mattered," Amy says. "He's the band/music director. He's pitching songs, too. It's difficult, being in the public eye. Being visible isn't always a kind experience. Gary told me, 'When you decide to quit, I may go for it again, but until then, I'm here.'"

For all the stepped-up pace of expanding her musical endeavors, Amy Grant is in some ways much the same person she was at fifteen, when Word Records first recognized the appeal of the open and vulnerable teen. Her mother sees the similarities, which have been reinforced in the protective environment of family, management, and creative partners (who often seem to blend into one category instead of three).

"Amy hasn't changed a lot," observes Gloria Grant. "She's grown a little older, and wiser. But she's always been a wise child for her age, always."

Her strength as an influential entertainer was demonstrated when she was able to get her audience to form a 10,000-person human wave, swaying to the rhythm of her songs at the Murphy Center homecoming concert. Amy demonstrates an image of almost childlike trust that inspires hero worship from adolescents and much goodwill

among older fans. Her crowds today are not as homoge-
neously Young Life Christian as the crowds she used to
draw in smaller numbers years earlier. Though their parents might wish otherwise, many younger Amy Grant fans
are also fans of older or bolder trends in popular music.

"My daughter is a big fan of Amy's," explained Nashville
advertising executive Bill Hudson at Amy's middle Tennessee homecoming appearance at Murfreesboro's Murphy
Center auditorium. "I thought I'd encourage this and
maybe she'd get less interested in Motley Crue."

With their parents' encouragement, a new generation of
fashion-conscious teenaged girls are the most rabid fans.
They find in Amy a caring big sister whose message says,
"Having fun is okay, nobody's perfect, and God loves them
anyway."

"I want them to know that being a Christian doesn't
mean that you have to stop enjoying life or become a nerd
and wear unstylish clothes," Amy says.

It is Amy's ministry, if you will, to give youngsters a taste
of Christianity made more appealing through the music of
their peers, letting ministers continue with the religious
specifics. Her musical theology is decidedly upbeat, light in
specific biblical content, and, by its Charismatic optimism,
a rebellion against the strict conservative religion of her
childhood. She is reaching young people with her message
because it rocks to the beat of pop music and because the
lyrics are hopeful and equate "being saved" with "being
happy."

"When I was fifteen I realized you didn't have to be a
clone," Amy says. "You're not going to be happy until you
accept yourself. That's been the theme of my songs for the
last nine years. My songs are half real and half hope. Don't
try to say something too heavy; just try to say something
that's hopeful. We've got to reach kids where they are right
now. We've got to get in there with whatever is communicating musically."

Even with the reduced emphasis on outright Inspirational music in her repertoire since "Unguarded" became her third album in a row to go gold in October 1985, Amy's positive religious faith projects from a stage with engaging magnetism. She is every bit as charismatic a personality to the age group she primarily addresses as Billy Graham is to his following. Her religious presentation ranges from the frothy entertainment of "Fat Baby" to the powerful and emotionally engaging "El Shaddai." Her audiences cheer her religious exhortations as passionately as they stomp out the rhythm of her upbeat melodies.

Despite detractors from some church-related groups and mocking by people who decidedly do not share the religious experience, Amy Grant definitely has star qualities. Her joy is tremendously infectious in concert and her record efforts have had an endearing tendency to get better with each outing. That she *is* a star, possibly on the verge of earning a permanent place in pop and adult contemporary radio, derives from the combined contributions of writers, musicians, tenacious management backed by strong family support, and, of course, her own talent. She continually points to stronger voices around her, but she is a first-rate entertainer who deserves her fame.

Amy has matured with her fame. She has stopped making pronouncements about when she and Gary will begin their family that marked her earlier self-effacing predictions about her longevity as an artist. One can't help feeling that Amy's clear sense of self will keep that goal in mind, though. Probably she will one day put her career on hold and take off a few years to start her family.

The strength of her faith and the size of her accomplishments might even suggest that in her old age, Amy Grant will have grandchildren and great-grandchildren around her own huge rural home, creating a Chapman Farm memory to inspire future generations of her staunchly religious and outgoing family, just as great-grandmother "Mimi" Burton did for Amy's generation so many years ago.

"Grandma Amy was a big star," that future generation will tell each other. They'll be right, but will they realize the meaning of the breakthrough she accomplished?

Amy Grant Discography

"Amy Grant"
    Myrrh/Word 1977, MSB-6586 (reissued with new
    cover art)
"My Father's Eyes"
    Myrrh/Word 1979, MSB-6625
"Never Alone"
    Myrrh/Word 1980, MSB-6645
"Amy Grant—In Concert"
    Myrrh/Word 1981, MSB-6668
"In Concert—Vol II"
    Myrrh/Word 1981, MSB-6677
"Age to Age"
    Myrrh/Word 1982, MSB-6697
"A Christmas Album"
    Myrrh/Word 1983, MSB-6768
"Straight Ahead"
    Myrrh/Word 1984, SPCN 7–01–675706–4
"Unguarded"
    Myrrh/Word/A&M 1985, SPCN 7–01–680606–5
Mini EP/LP "Ageless Medley"
    Myrrh/Word 1983, M001EP

Guest appearance on: DeGarmo and Key LP
"This Ain't Hollywood"
    Lamb & Lion 1980, LL-1051

Guest appearance on: Gary Chapman LP
"Sincerely Yours"
    Lamb & Lion 1981, LL-1053

Guest appearance on: Gary Chapman LP
"Happenin' "
    Lamb & Lion 1982, LL-1066 (out of print)

Guest appearance on: Michael W. Smith LP
"Michael W. Smith Project"
    Reunion/Word 1983, RRA 0002

Guest appearance on: Michael W. Smith LP
"Michael W. Smith 2"
    Reunion/Word 1984, 7-01-000412-9

Guest appearance on: the gospel famine relief record
"Do Something Now"
    Christian Artists United to Save the Earth Sparrow
    1985, SGL 1110

Guest appearance on: Randy Stonehill LP
"Love Beyond Reason"
    Myrrh-L.A./Word 1985, 7-01-681106-9

Guest appearance on: special television compilation
"Sing Your Praises to the Lord"
    various artists
    Christian Broadcasting Network/Word 1985

Amy Grant's
Awards

1982   NARAS Grammy Award—Best Gospel Performance, Contemporary, "Age to Age"

1983   GMA Dove Award—Contemporary Gospel Album of the Year, "Age to Age"

1983   GMA Dove Award—Gospel Artist of the Year

1983   NARAS Grammy Award—Best Gospel Performance, Female, "Ageless Medley" (single)

1984   NARAS Grammy Award—Best Gospel Performance, Female, "Angels" (from LP "Straight Ahead")

1985   GMA Dove Award—Gospel Music Album of the Year, Contemporary, "Straight Ahead"

1985   NARAS Grammy Award—Best Gospel Performance—Female, "Unguarded"

1986   GMA Dove Award—Gospel Artist of the Year

Amy Grant also received a number of award certificates from the American Society of Composers and Publishers (ASCAP) commemorating each of her GMA Dove Awards and Dove Award nominations through the years, the sole criterion for ASCAP Gospel Awards, which are presented at a luncheon hosted for the industry by the performing rights organization during Gospel Music Week in Nashville each spring. In addition to numerous annual gospel music superlatives conferred by music trade magazines, Amy was nominated as Top New Country Vocalist—Female in the Academy of Country Music Hat Awards in 1983 for her single "Tennessee Christmas" and in the Gospel Act category of the 1984 and 1985 *Music City News* Awards.

Awards won by others in connection with Amy's records:

1981   GMA Dove Award—Gospel Songwriter of the Year,
        in part for "Father's Eyes" (from "My Father's Eyes")
        Gary Chapman

1983   GMA Dove Award—Gospel Song of the Year,
        "El Shaddai" (from "Age to Age") writers
        Michael Card
        John Thompson

1983   GMA Dove Award—Gospel Songwriter of the Year,
        Michael Card
        (cowriter of "El Shaddai")

1983   GMA Dove Award—Gospel Record Album Cover of the Year, "Age to Age"
        designer, Dennis Hill
        photographer, Michael Borum

1984   GMA Dove Award—Gospel Music Album of the Year—Design,
        "A Christmas Album"
        art director, Dennis Hill
        photographers, Bill Farrell, Michael Borum

1985   GMA Dove Award—Gospel Music Album of the
Year,
        Contemporary, "Straight Ahead"
        producer, Brown Bannister

1986   GMA Dove Award—Gospel Album of the Year—
Design,
        "Unguarded"
        photography, Mark Tucker
        graphics, Kent Hunter

Brown Bannister has won five Doves:

1981   Song of the Year "Praise The Lord" (as writer
        with Mike Hudson)
1981   LP of the Year by a Secular Artist "With My
        Song," D. Boone as producer
1983   Contemporary LP of the Year "Age to Age," as
        producer
1984   LP of the Year by a Secular Artist "Surrender,"
        D. Boone as producer
1985   Contemporary LP of the Year "Straight Ahead,"
        as producer